Test Yourself

Abnormal Psychology

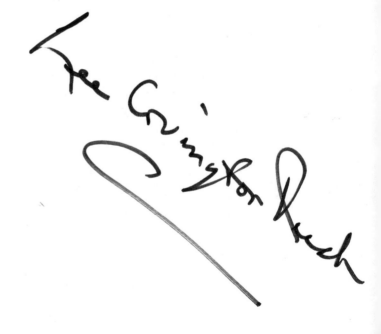

Susanna M. Perry, Ph.D.
Department of Psychology and Sociology
Texas A&M International University
Laredo, TX

Contributing Editors

Joseph J. Plaud, Ph.D.
Department of Psychology
University of North Dakota
Grand Forks, ND

Lisa Terre, Ph.D.
Department of Psychology
University of Missouri–Kansas City
Kansas City, MO

John M. Schuster, Ph.D.
Counseling Center
Texas Christian University
Ft. Worth, TX

NTC LEARNINGWORKS
NTC/Contemporary Publishing Group

Library of Congress Cataloging-in-Publication Data
Perry, Susanna M.
     Abnormal psychology / Susanna M. Perry.
         p.   cm. — (Test yourself)
     ISBN 0-8442-2384-0
     1. Psychology, Pathological—Examinations, questions, etc.
I. Title. II. Series: Test yourself (Lincolnwood, Ill.)
RC454.P43   1998
616.89′0076—dc21   98-23395
                                      CIP

A *Test Yourself Books, Inc.* Project

Published by NTC LearningWorks
A division of NTC/Contemporary Publishing Group, Inc.
4255 West Touhy Avenue, Lincolnwood (Chicago), Illinois 60646-1975 U.S.A.
Copyright © 1999 by NTC/Contemporary Publishing Group, Inc.
All rights reserved. No part of this book may be reproduced, stored
in a retrieval system, or transmitted in any form or by any means,
electronic, mechanical, photocopying, recording, or otherwise, without
the prior permission of NTC/Contemporary Publishing Group, Inc.
Printed in the United States of America
International Standard Book Number: 0-8442-2384-0
18 17 16 15 14 13 12 11 10 9 8 7 6 5 4 3 2 1

Contents

Preface

Since you are reading this book, you are probably trying to earn better grades in your Abnormal Psychology class. This text was written with that in mind, in order to facilitate your learning and retention of the information covered. Abnormal psychology has an immense span, covering all types of recognized mental disorders. My goal was to illustrate and explain each disorder in an easy and comprehensive manner. You may feel somewhat overwhelmed by the breadth and diversity of material, but that is only natural. Once you begin to understand the concepts involved, new material will be understood more readily.

This text is designed to accompany any other textbook in this field, so it is fairly general in nature. I would suggest reading it along with your assigned text. Although it may seem redundant, this rehearsal is what will enable you to retain the information necessary to excel on exams. It might also be helpful to study with others in order to clarify things you may not understand. The main point is that you must use the information provided in some way so that you will understand each concept.

This book describes psychological disorders, theoretical perspectives on the etiology of abnormality, the historical perspective, and treatments for psychological disorders. You may be surprised by what you learn. For instance, most people have a misconception about the nature of schizophrenia. The term originally meant "split-mind," yet today it is used to describe a psychoses which manifests itself in delusions and hallucinations. It does not mean having a split personality although many people still believe this today. We have many stereotypes about the mentally ill, and hopefully you will begin to question these stereotypes and begin to look at the research evidence instead of these preconceived notions. It is also important to remember that psychological disorders are culture-bound. This means that they are behaviors determined by a particular culture to be different from what is expected. Some people see extreme behavior as abnormal, while others see norm violations as normal. Abnormality can be, and is, defined in different ways by different people, so it is important to keep in mind that this field is not black and white.

Susanna M. Perry, Ph.D.

How to Use This Book

This "Test Yourself" book is part of a unique series designed to help you improve your test scores on almost any type of examination you will face. Too often, you will study for a test—quiz, midterm, or final—and come away with a score that is lower than anticipated. Why? Because there is no way for you to really know how much you understand a topic until you've taken a test. The *purpose* of the test, after all, is to test your complete understanding of the material.

The "Test Yourself" series offers you a way to improve your scores and to actually test your knowledge at the time you use this book. Consider each chapter a diagnostic pretest in a specific topic. Answer the questions, check your answers, and then give yourself a grade. Then, and only then, will you know where your strengths and, more important, weaknesses are. Once these areas are identified, you can strategically focus your study on those topics that need additional work.

Each book in this series presents a specific subject in an organized manner, and although each "Test Yourself" chapter may not correspond to exactly the same chapter in your textbook, you should have little difficulty in locating the specific topic you are studying. Written by educators in the field, each book is designed to correspond, as much as possible, to the leading textbooks. This means that you can feel confident in using this book and that regardless of your textbook, professor, or school, you will be much better prepared for anything you will encounter on your test.

Each chapter has four parts:

Brief Yourself. All chapters contain a brief overview of the topic that is intended to give you a more thorough understanding of the material with which you need to be familiar. Sometimes this information is presented at the beginning of the chapter, and sometimes it flows throughout the chapter, to review your understanding of various *units* within the chapter.

Test Yourself. Each chapter covers a specific topic corresponding to one that you will find in your textbook. Answer the questions, either on a separate page or directly in the book, if there is room.

Check Yourself. Check your answers. Every question is fully answered and explained. These answers will be the key to your increased understanding. If you answered the question incorrectly, read the explanations to *learn* and *understand* the material. You will note that at the end of every answer you will be referred to a specific subtopic within that chapter, so you can focus your studying and prepare more efficiently.

Grade Yourself. At the end of each chapter is a self-diagnostic key. By indicating on this form the numbers of those questions you answered incorrectly, you will have a clear picture of your weak areas.

There are no secrets to test success. Only good preparation can guarantee higher grades. By utilizing this "Test Yourself" book, you will have a better chance of improving your scores and understanding the subject more fully.

History of Psychopathology

1

Brief Yourself

The study of psychopathology is an examination of why people behave, think, and feel in unusual, surprising and even bizarre ways. The study of psychopathology has its origins in demonology. There are two opposing views on psychopathology: the *somatogenic*, which assumes that mental illnesses are due to physical malfunction; and the *psychogenic*, which assumes that mental difficulties are explained in psychological terms. Various theories make assumptions about the nature of abnormal behavior but do not explicitly define it. There are many definitions of abnormality, but no single one is fully adequate. The various parameters for determining abnormality are statistical, subjective distress, impaired functioning, and norm violations.

Test Yourself

Define the terms in questions 1–7.

1. Demonology

2. Somatogenic perspective

3. Psychogenic perspective

4. Asylums

5. Syndrome

6. Dementia praecox

7. Abreaction

Questions 8–19 are true-false.

8. Babylonians believed that a specific demon was responsible for each disease.

9. Hippocrates was viewed as the father of modern medicine because he separated religion from magic and superstition.

10. Hippocrates was the earliest proponent of the psychogenic view.

11. During the Dark Ages all mentally ill people were believed to be witches.

12. According to Hippocrates, too much blood was responsible for melancholia.

13. By the end of the Crusades there were mental hospitals all over Europe.

14. The hospitalization of mental patients led to more humane treatment of the mentally ill.

15. Beginning in the thirteenth century, trials determined a person's sanity in England.

16. Rush thought mental patients were essentially normal people who needed treatment that included compassion and dignity.

17. Kraeplin developed the first modern classification system to help establish the organic basis of mental disorders.

18. Kraeplin believed that there were three categories of mental disorders: mania, melancholia, and phrenitis.

19. Breuer used hypnotism to treat Anna O.

20. What is demonology and what does it have to do with abnormal behavior?

21. Who was first to separate medicine from superstition?

22. What did Hippocrates believe about abnormal behavior?

23. What is meant by the "somatogenic hypothesis"?

24. How did Hippocrates classify mental disorders?

25. How did Hippocrates conceptualize brain functioning?

26. What impact did the Dark Ages have on the mentally ill?

27. What does witchcraft have to do with mental illness?

28. How was a person's sanity determined during the Middle Ages?

29. What are asylums and when did they arise in response to mental illness?

30. Did the advent of asylums lead to more humane treatment of the mentally ill?

31. Who was the first advocate of humane treatment of the mentally disturbed?

32. Who were early proponents of the somatogenic model?

33. Discuss Kraeplin's classification system.

34. Discuss the origin of the psychogenic view of mental illness.

35. Who were early proponents of the psychogenic view and how did their ideas affect the treatment of the mentally ill?

36. What is abnormal?

 # Check Yourself

1. *Demonology* refers to a belief that an evil being lives within a person and controls his or her mind and behavior. **(Definitions)**

2. The *somatogenic perspective* states that in a mentally ill person there must be something wrong with the physical body that is causing the disturbance. **(Definitions)**

3. The *psychogenic perspective* believes that mental illness is due to psychological malfunctions. **(Definitions)**

4. *Asylums* arose after the Crusades to hospitalize the mentally ill. **(Definitions)**

5. A *syndrome* is a group of symptoms that naturally occur together. **(Definitions)**

6. *Dementia praecox* was the early term used for schizophrenia by Kraeplin. **(Definitions)**

7. *Abreaction* refers to the release of the emotional tension that follows the recollection and reexperiencing of an emotional trauma. (**Definitions**)

8. **True.** Babylonians believed that a specific demon was responsible for each disease. (**History of psychopathology**)

9. **False.** Hippocrates was viewed as the father of modern medicine because he separated *medicine* from *magic and superstition*. (**History of psychopathology**)

10. **False.** Hippocrates was the earliest proponent of the *somatogenic* view. (**History of psychopathology**)

11. **False.** During the *Middle Ages, some* mentally ill people were believed to be witches. (**History of psychopathology**)

12. **False.** According to Hippocrates, too much blood was responsible for *mood changes*. (**History of psychopathology**)

13. **False.** By the end of the Crusades, there were *few* mental hospitals in Europe. (**History of psychopathology**)

14. **False.** The hospitalization of mental patients *did not* lead to more humane treatment of the mentally ill. (**History of psychopathology**)

15. **True.** Beginning in the thirteenth century, trials determined a person's sanity in England. (**History of psychopathology**)

16. **False.** *Pinel* thought mental patients were essentially normal people who needed treatment that included compassion and dignity. (**History of psychopathology**)

17. **True.** Kraeplin developed the first modern classification system to help establish the organic basis of mental disorders. (**History of psychopathology**)

18. **False.** Kraeplin believed that there were two groups of mental disorders: *dementia praecox* and *manic-depressive psychosis*. (**History of psychopathology**)

19. **True.** Breuer used hypnotism to treat Anna O. (**History of psychopathology**)

20. Demonology refers to a belief or doctrine that an autonomous evil being, such as the devil, lives within a person and controls his or her mind and body. The ancient Babylonians believed that a specific demon was responsible for each disease. Similar examples of such beliefs occurred in the cultures of the ancient Chinese, Egyptians, and Greeks. Treatment tried to exorcise these demons. Treatment thus consisted of prayer rituals, drinking potions, or such extreme things as flogging and starvation. (**History of psychopathology**)

21. Hippocrates is considered the father of modern medicine because he separated medicine from religion and superstition. He also rejected the prevailing Greek belief that the gods sent serious physical and mental disturbances as punishment. Hippocrates insisted that mental disturbances were naturally caused and could be treated like other diseases. (**History of psychopathology**)

22. Hippocrates believed that the brain was the organ of consciousness, of intellectual life, and emotion. Thus, he believed that if someone's thinking and behavior were abnormal, there must be some kind of brain pathology. (**History of psychopathology**)

23.   Hippocrates was the earliest proponent of the view that attempted to explain abnormal behavior. The hypothesis stated that, in a disordered person, there must be something wrong with the *soma,* or physical body, that disturbs mental processes. However, Hippocrates also realized that environmental and emotional stress can also impact the physical body and the mind. (**History of psychopathology**)

24.   Hippocrates believed that there were three categories of mental disorders: mania, melancholia, and phrenitis, or brain fever. It was through the teachings of Hippocrates that mental disorders became a medical matter for physicians rather than priests. (**History of psychopathology**)

25.   Hippocrates believed that mental health was dependent upon a balance among four bodily fluids. These fluids were blood, black bile, yellow bile, and phlegm. Melancholia was the result of an excess of black bile, excess yellow bile resulted in anxiety, and excess blood caused mood changes. His belief was that human behavior is influenced by bodily substances. Thus, abnormal behavior was the result of an imbalance of these fluids. (**History of psychopathology**)

26.   During the Dark Ages, the mentally ill were cared for in monasteries. The monks treated them by praying for them, touching them with relics, or making potions for them to drink. Many mentally ill were homeless and became more disturbed with the passage of time. (**History of psychopathology**)

27.   In the latter part of the Middle Ages, some mentally disturbed people were considered to be witches. Although there were some alleged witches that were mentally disturbed, there were many more undisturbed people who were considered witches. Witchcraft or possession was only one explanation for mental disturbances and was not the primary explanation. (**History of psychopathology**)

28.   During this time, some European laws provided for the hospitalization of the mentally disturbed. Beginning in the thirteenth century, trials determined a person's sanity in England. The judgment of insanity allowed the Crown to become guardian of the person's estate. This trial examined the person's orientation, memory, intellect, daily functioning, and habits. The explanations for abnormality were related to physical illness or emotional trauma. (**History of psychopathology**)

29.   Until the end of the Crusades, there were virtually no mental hospitals in Europe. The advent of the sixteenth century brought about serious attempts to place the mentally disturbed in asylums. Some of these asylums took in the poor as well as the mentally ill. (**History of psychopathology**)

30.   The inclusion of mental patients in hospitals did not necessarily lead to more humane treatment of the mentally ill. Benjamin Rush, the father of American psychiatry, believed that mental disorder was due to an excess of blood in the brain. His treatment consisted of taking large amounts of blood from the mentally disturbed person. Rush also believed that lunatics could be cured by frightening them. (**History of psychopathology**)

31.   Phillippe Pinel was a major figure in the movement to treat the mentally ill more humanely. He was in charge of a French asylum during the French Revolution. Pinel removed the shackles of patients and treated them as sick human beings rather than animals. Light and airy rooms replaced dungeons. Pinel thought mental patients were essentially normal people who needed treatment that included compassion and dignity. He believed their reason might return to them through comforting counsel and meaningful activity. (**History of psychopathology**)

32. Physicians advocated an empirical approach to classification and physiological causes as the underlying factors in mental disorders. A textbook of psychiatry first published in 1883 by Emil Kraeplin furnished a classification system to help establish the organic basis of mental disorders. Kraeplin found that there was a tendency for a group of symptoms, referred to as a syndrome, to co-occur regularly enough to be conceptualized as having an underlying physical cause. He regarded each mental illness as unique, each having its own cause, symptoms, and prognosis. **(History of psychopathology)**

33. Kraeplin proposed two major groups of severe mental disorders: dementia praecox and manic-depressive psychosis. Dementia praecox was an early term for schizophrenia. He thought that a chemical imbalance caused schizophrenia and an irregularity in metabolism caused manic-depressive psychosis. Kraeplin's classification system became the basis for modern diagnostic categories. **(History of psychopathology)**

34. Although most psychiatrists focused on somatogenic causes, in parts of Western Europe, some believed that mental disturbances were psychogenic in origin. Psychogenic proponents argued that mental illness was attributable to psychic malfunctions. Many people at this time suffered from hysteria (now termed conversion disorders), which had no apparent physical basis. Mesmer believed that hysterical disorders were due to a specific distribution of magnetic fluid in the body. He believed that one person could influence the fluid in another person's body causing changes in that person's behavior. Mesmer was an early practitioner of hypnosis. **(History of psychopathology)**

35. Josef Breuer's patient, Anna O., had many hysterical symptoms. She suffered from paralysis and impaired vision, hearing and speech. Breuer hypnotized her. He succeeded in getting her to talk more freely and upon awakening she frequently felt better. Breuer found symptoms were relieved if the patient could remember what originally caused the symptom. This reliving of an earlier emotional trauma and the release of the emotional tension was called abreaction or catharsis. Breuer's method became known as the cathartic method. **(History of psychopathology)**

36. Various theories of psychopathology all make assumptions about abnormal behavior, yet many fail to define exactly what abnormality is. There are several definitions for abnormal behavior. One definition of abnormal is that it is statistically infrequent behavior. Most people behave in ways that are typical or average. Very few people exhibit extreme behaviors. Extreme behaviors are statistically infrequent, so they qualify as abnormal. However, not all kinds of infrequent behavior are considered to be pathological. The statistical definition does not tell us which kinds of infrequent behavior ought to be considered abnormal or pathological. Another definition of abnormal encompasses subjective distress. If a person's behavior causes them emotional distress, then it is abnormal. However, some disorders cause little distress to the person with the disorder, like the antisocial personality disorder, in which the person behaves without feeling guilt, remorse, or anxiety. Another difficulty with this definition is that it is entirely subjective, each individual reporting his or her own level of distress. This subjectivity makes comparisons to others futile. Sometimes the definition of abnormal is based on whether a person's social or occupational functioning is impaired. Definitions of abnormal behavior may also involve violating social rules, such as engaging in criminal behavior. This definition makes abnormality a relative concept varying by culture and time. Another way of defining abnormality is as behavior which is self-destructive or dangerous (to oneself and/or others). We have multiple definitions of abnormality, yet not one is sufficient to cover the range of psychological disorders. Perhaps a good definition would include all the aforementioned attributes. Abnormal behavior is behavior that is extreme, causes distress, results in impaired functioning, and violates prevailing social norms. **(What is abnormal)**

Grade Yourself

Circle the numbers of the questions you missed, then fill in the total incorrect for each topic. If you answered more than three questions incorrectly, you need to focus on that topic. (If a topic has fewer than three questions and you had at least one wrong, we suggest you study that topic also. Read your textbook or a review book, or ask your teacher for help.)

Subject: History of Psychopathology

Topic	Question Numbers	Number Incorrect
Definitions	1, 2, 3, 4, 5, 6, 7	
History of psychopathology	8, 9, 10, 11, 12, 13, 14, 15, 16, 17, 18, 19, 20, 21, 22, 23, 24, 25, 26, 27, 28, 29, 30, 31, 32, 33, 34, 35	
What is abnormal	36	

Theoretical Approaches to Abnormal Psychology

2

Brief Yourself

This chapter deals with the various theoretical models used to conceptualize abnormal behavior, how it develops, and the best ways to treat abnormal behavior. Five major theoretical views will be discussed: the *physiological* approach, the *psychoanalytic* approach, *learning* approach, the *cognitive* approach, and the *humanistic* approach. The choice of which approach a particular clinician adopts is important because it drives assumptions about the causes and treatment of psychological disorders. The physiological approach proposes that abnormal behavior is like a disease, the result of dysfunctional physiological processes. The psychoanalytic approach is based on the work of Sigmund Freud and postulates that unconscious sexual and aggressive drives motivate our behavior. Since Freud, some neo-Freudians like Carl Jung, Alfred Adler, and Erik Erikson have modified original psychoanalytic theory. The learning approach contains two different perspectives: the classical and operant conditioning perspectives. The classical conditioning approach involves the pairing of stimuli while the operant approach emphasizes the effects of consequences on behavior. The cognitive approach sees human behavior as more complex than simple stimulus-response associations and regards people as active learners. The humanistic approach is a reaction against the psychoanalytic approach that has dominated much of psychology since Freud's era. The humanistic view holds that people are basically good, have free will and have a drive toward self-actualization. Currently, psychological disorders are believed to be the result of the interaction of biological, pscyhological, and social factors.

Test Yourself

Define the terms in questions 1–39.

1. Medical model

2. Id

3. Ego

4. Superego

5. Primary process thinking

6. Secondary process thinking

7. Pleasure principle

8. Reality principle

9. Eros

10. Thanatos

11. Libido

12. Oedipus complex

13. Neurotic anxiety

14. Objective anxiety

15. Moral anxiety

16. Defense mechanisms

17. Repression

18. Reaction Formation

19. Displacement

20. Projection

21. Regression

22. Collective unconscious

23. Individual psychology

24. Free association

25. Dream analysis

26. Classical conditioning

27. UCS

28. UCR

29. CS

30. CR

31. Law of Effect

32. Operant conditioning

33. Counterconditioning

34. Cognitive-behavior therapy

35. Client-centered therapy

36. Empathy

37. Unconditional positive regard

38. Genuineness

39. RET

Questions 40–72 are true-false.

40. The medical model refers to the psychoanalytic approach to psychopathology.

41. Surgery and drugs are typical treatments recommended by the physiological approach.

42. Freud developed the psychoanalytic approach which focused on unconscious determinants of behavior, such as aggressive and sexual impulses.

43. The ego is considered to be the conscience.

44. The id is the most advanced structure of the mind.

45. The ego operates on the pleasure principle.

46. The superego develops through resolution of the Oedipus complex.

47. Within the ego are the life and death instincts.

48. Primary process thinking occurs when the id generates images of desired objects.

49. Secondary process thinking occurs when the superego plans behavior.

50. The ego is primarily conscious.

51. The id is primarily unconscious.

52. The first stage of psychosexual development is the anal stage.

53. The period between stages marked by a psychologically calm period is called the latency period.

54. When a person remains stuck at a particular stage due to excess or insufficient gratification, it is called fixation.

55. The final psychosexual stage is the genital stage in which homosexual interests predominate.

56. Neurotic anxiety is guilt that results from the fear of punishment for failing to adhere to the superego's moral standards.

57. Defense mechanisms are conscious strategies used to protect the ego from anxiety.

58. Projection is a defense mechanism that attributes to others unacceptable characteristics or desires possessed by an individual.

59. Repression refers to returning to the behaviors of an earlier developmental period.

60. Freud believed that we have a collective unconscious, which contains information from mankind's social history.

61. Adler focused on the need to strive for superiority.

62. Erikson emphasized the development of ego identity.

63. Psychoanalytic therapy tries to help patients remove repression and face childhood conflicts in order to resolve that conflict.

64. The best known psychoanalytic technique is dream analysis, which encourages patients to say whatever comes to mind without censorship.

65. Classical conditioning is learning that two stimuli are associated and responding to the conditioned stimulus according to Skinner.

66. Operant conditioning began with the work of Edward Thorndike, who proposed that behavior that is followed by satisfying consequences will be repeated.

67. Counterconditioning may help treat phobias by replacing a fear response with a non-fear response to a specific stimulus.

68. Cognitive-behavior therapists try to alter the thought processes of clients in order to change their emotions and behavior.

69. Adler's therapy, rational emotive therapy, makes patients challenge irrational beliefs and substitute rational thoughts.

70. Maslow believed that people are basically healthy and are driven toward self-actualization.

71. The three conditions necessary for effective treatment in client-centered therapy are empathy, unconditional positive regard, and repression.

72. What is the physiological approach to abnormality?

73. What kinds of treatment are typical of the physiological approach?

74. What is the psychoanalytic approach?

75. Discuss Freud's structure of the mind.

76. What are the psychosexual stages of development?

77. What is the most important crisis of development in Freudian theory?

78. Discuss Freud's conceptualization of anxiety.

79. What are defense mechanisms?

80. What changes to psychoanalytic theory did Carl Jung make?

81. How did Alfred Adler modify Freud's theory?

82. Discuss Erik Erikson's ego psychology.

83. What are the major premises of psychoanalytic therapy?

84. What are some techniques used by psychoanalysts?

85. What is classical conditioning?

86. How does operant conditioning differ from classical conditioning?

87. What is modeling?

88. Discuss counterconditioning.

89. What is the cognitive approach?

90. Discuss the major premises of cognitive-behavior therapy.

91. Compare and contrast humanism with behaviorism.

92. Describe client-centered therapy.

93. Describe the biopsychosocial approach.

 # Check Yourself

1. The physiological approach which views abnormal behavior much like a disease is often referred to as the *medical model*. (**Definitions**)

2. The *id*, which is present at birth, is the most primitive of these psychic structures and operates on the pleasure principle, seeking immediate gratification. (**Definitions**)

3. The second personality structure is the *ego*, which is primarily conscious and arises from the id. The ego must deal with reality and operates on the reality principle. (**Definitions**)

4. The *superego* is the third aspect of personality and it develops through resolution of the Oedipus conflict. The superego represents an internalization of the societal standards of morality. (**Definitions**)

5. *Primary process thinking* is used by the id to generate mental images of the desired object. (**Definitions**)

6. *Secondary process thinking* is used by the ego in planning and decision making. (**Definitions**)

7. The id operates on the *pleasure principle* to achieve immediate gratification of impulses. (**Definitions**)

8. The *reality principle* is used by the ego to mediate between the id and the external environment. (**Definitions**)

9. *Eros* is life instinct, or drive, which is primarily sexual. (**Definitions**)

10. *Thanatos* is the death instinct in psychoanalytic theory. (**Definitions**)

11. *Libido* is the energy of Eros. (**Definitions**)

12. The *Oedipus complex* occurs in the phallic stage when the child experiences sexual desire for the opposite-sex parent and fears punishment from the same-sex parent which may lead to repression. This conflict is resolved by identification with the same-sex parent and internalization of moral standards. (**Definitions**)

13. *Neurotic anxiety* is the fear of unpleasant consequences that are thought to follow if an unacceptable id impulse is expressed. (**Definitions**)

14. *Objective anxiety* refers to the ego's reaction to actual danger. **(Definitions)**

15. *Moral anxiety* is guilt or shame for failing to adhere to moral principles. **(Definitions)**

16. *Defense mechanisms* are unconscious strategies used to protect the ego from anxiety. **(Definitions)**

17. *Repression occurs* when unacceptable desires or traumatic events are pushed into the unconscious. **(Definitions)**

18. *Reaction formation* is a defense mechanism that converts an unacceptable feeling into its opposite. **(Definitions)**

19. *Displacement* is a defense mechanism in which a person redirects emotional responses from a dangerous object to a safer substitute. **(Definitions)**

20. *Projection* is a defense mechanism in which people attribute unacceptable desires possessed by themselves onto other people. **(Definitions)**

21. *Regression* is a defense mechanism that involves retreating into an earlier developmental state. **(Definitions)**

22. Jung believed that we all have a universal *collective unconscious* which contains information about human history. **(Definitions)**

23. *Individual psychology* refers to Alfred Adler's psychology that focuses on a striving for superiority and a social interest. **(Definitions)**

24. *Free association* is a psychoanalytic technique used to recover repressed memories by encouraging the patient to speak freely, without censorship, about whatever comes to mind. **(Definitions)**

25. *Dream analysis* is another psychoanalytic technique that focuses on analyzing the symbolic content of dreams to uncover repressed impulses. **(Definitions)**

26. *Classical conditioning* is a form of learning which was described by Ivan Pavlov and involves the contingent pairing of a previously neutral stimulus with an unconditioned stimulus to elicit a conditioned response. **(Definitions)**

27. The *UCS* is a stimulus that naturally elicits a response, such as the meat powder in Pavlov's experiment. **(Definitions)**

28. The *UCR* is a response that occurs naturally to a UCS, like salivation to the meat powder in Pavlov's experiment. **(Definitions)**

29. The *CS* is a previously neutral stimulus that is paired with the UCS in order to elicit a response. The CS in Pavlov's experiment was the bell. **(Definitions)**

30. The *CR* is a learned response that occurs after repeated pairings of the UCS and CS. In Pavlov's experiment, the CR is salivation to the sound of the bell. **(Definitions)**

31. The *law of effect* proposed by Thorndike states that a behavior that is followed by satisfying consequences will reoccur. **(Definitions)**

32. *Operant conditioning* refers to learning that occurs when a response is followed by either a reinforcer or punisher. Skinner thought that a behavior's recurrence is determined by the consequence that follows the behavior. Positively reinforced behaviors tend to increase, while punished behavior decreases. Skinner and other operant theorists stressed the importance of positive reinforcement in behavior shaping and maintenance. **(Definitions)**

33. *Counterconditioning* involves eliminating a response to a stimulus by eliciting a new response in the presence of the same stimulus. **(Definitions)**

34. *Cognitive-behavior therapy* attempts to modify the thought processes of clients in order to change their emotions and behavior. **(Definitions)**

35. *Client-centered therapy* was developed by Carl Rogers. The person seeking therapy is a client rather than a patient and is responsible for the course of his or her treatment. Therapists create conditions that help clients discover their feelings and make their own decisions about what they need. This reflects a shift from a medical perspective to a psychological perspective. **(Definitions)**

36. *Empathy* involves being able to take the perspective of the clients. **(Definitions)**

37. *Unconditional positive regard* means that the therapist accepts the client as a person worthy of dignity and respect, regardless of his or her behavior. **(Definitions)**

38. *Genuineness* is communicated by the therapist who is honest and willing to share some of his or her own experiences when necessary. **(Definitions)**

39. Ellis's therapy, *rational emotive therapy (RET)*, helps patients challenge their beliefs and teaches them how to substitute rational thoughts. **(Definitions)**

40. False. The medical model refers to the *physiological* approach to psychopathology. **(Physiological approach)**

41. **True.** Surgery and drugs are typical treatments recommended by the physiological approach. **(Physiological approach)**

42. **True.** Freud developed the psychoanalytic approach, which focuses on unconscious determinants of behavior, such as aggressive and sexual impulses. **(Psychoanalytic approach)**

43. **False.** The *superego* is considered to be the conscience. **(Psychoanalytic approach)**

44. **False.** The id is the most *primitive* structure of the mind. **(Psychoanalytic approach)**

45. **False.** The ego operates on the *reality* principle. **(Psychoanalytic approach)**

46. **True.** The superego develops through resolution of the Oedipus complex. **(Psychoanalytic approach)**

47. **False.** Within the *id* are the life and death instincts. **(Psychoanalytic approach)**

48. **True.** Primary process thinking occurs when the id generates images of desired objects. **(Psychoanalytic approach)**

49. **False.** Secondary process thinking occurs when the *ego* plans behavior. **(Psychoanalytic approach)**

50. **True.** The ego is primarily conscious. (**Psychoanalytic approach**)

51. **True.** The id is primarily unconscious. (**Psychoanalytic approach**)

52. **False.** The first stage of psychosexual development is the *oral* stage. (**Psychoanalytic approach**)

53. **True.** The period between stages marked by "emotional" calm is called the latency period. (**Psychoanalytic approach**)

54. **True.** When a person remains stuck at a particular stage due to excess or insufficient gratification, it is called fixation. (**Psychoanalytic approach**)

55. **False.** The final psychosexual stage is the genital stage in which *heterosexual* interests predominate. (**Psychoanalytic approach**)

56. **False.** *Moral* anxiety is guilt that results from the fear of punishment for failing to adhere to the superego's moral standards. (**Psychoanalytic approach**)

57. **False.** Defense mechanisms are *unconscious* processes used to protect the ego from anxiety. (**Psychoanalytic approach**)

58. **True.** Projection is a defense mechanism that attributes to others unacceptable characteristics possessed by an individual. (**Psychoanalytic approach**)

59. **False.** *Regression* refers to returning to the behaviors of an earlier developmental period. (**Psychoanalytic approach**)

60. **False.** *Jung* believed that we have a collective unconscious, which contains information from mankind's social history. (**Psychoanalytic approach**)

61. **True.** Adler focused on the need to strive for superiority. (**Psychoanalytic approach**)

62. **True.** Erikson emphasized the development of ego identity. (**Psychoanalytic approach**)

63. **True.** Psychoanalytic therapy tries to help patients remove repression and face childhood conflicts in order to resolve that conflict. (**Psychoanalytic approach**)

64. **False.** One of the best known psychoanalytic techniques is *free association*, which encourages patients to say whatever comes to mind, without censorship. (**Psychoanalytic approach**)

65. **False.** Classical conditioning is pairing a neutral stimulus with a response until the neutral stimulus elicits the response, according to *Pavlov*. (**Learning approach**)

66. **True.** Operant conditioning began with the work of Edward Thorndike who proposed that behavior that is followed by satisfying consequences will be repeated. (**Learning approach**)

67. True. Counterconditioning may help treat phobias by replacing a fear response with a non-fear response to a specific stimulus. (**Learning approach**)

68. True. Cognitive-behavior therapists try to alter the thought processes of clients in order to change their emotions and behavior. (**Cognitive approach**)

69. False. *Ellis's* therapy, rational emotive behavior therapy (REBT), makes patients challenge irrational beliefs and substitute rational thoughts. (**Cognitive approach**)

70. True. Maslow believed that people are basically healthy and are driven toward self-actualization. (**Humanistic approach**)

71. **False.** The three conditions necessary for effective treatment in client-centered therapy are empathy, unconditional positive regard, and *genuineness*. (**Humanistic approach**)

72. The physiological approach views abnormal behavior much like a disease. This approach is often called the *medical model*. Abnormal behavior is caused by disruptions in physiological processes. (**Physiological approach**)

73. An implication of the physiological approach is that surgery or drugs may be effective in treating psychological disorders. There are physiological interventions that we use because we know that they relieve symptoms. Sedatives are effective in treating anxiety disorders yet we are uncertain about what causes anxiety disorders. (**Physiological approach**)

74. Sigmund Freud developed psychoanalytic theory and the psychoanalytic approach to therapy. Freud proposed a theory of personality development and stages of psychosexual development. Freud believed that the most important determinants of behavior are unconscious. Also, Freud believed that behavior is the result of a complex interaction between our id, ego, and superego. (**Psychoanalytic approach**)

75. Freud believed that the mind consists of three major parts: the id, ego, and superego. Each part has specific rules and has specific duties. These are not actual brain structures but are psychological constructs used to explain personality development. The first is the *id* which is present at birth and is the most primitive of these structures. The id contains most basic urges such as hunger, thirst, warmth, and sex. Within the id are the life instincts (*Eros*) and death instincts (*Thanatos*). Eros is a life force, primarily sexual. The energy of Eros is the *libido*. Thanatos is the death instinct. The id seeks immediate gratification and operates on the *pleasure principle*. If the id cannot satisfy a need immediately, the id may engage in *primary process* thinking, generating mental images of the desired object. The second psychic structure is the *ego* and it is primarily conscious. The ego develops from the id at about the age of six months. The ego operates on the reality principle, which means that the ego mediates between the demands of reality and the id. The ego uses *secondary process* thinking, which involves planning and decision making. The ego must also mediate between reality and the superego. The *superego* is the third mental structure. The superego develops through resolution of the Oedipus conflict and is what we call the conscience. The superego carries internalized societal standards of morality. (**Psychoanalytic approach**)

76. Freud proposed that personality develops through a series of psychosexual stages. At each stage a different part of the body is the most sensitive to sexual stimulation. In the first stage, the oral stage, the infant derives gratification from oral activities such as sucking and feeding. During the second year of life, the infant enters the anal stage. At this time, pleasure centers on the anus and elimination or retention of excrement. From age three to five, the child is in the phallic stage in which gratification comes from genital stimulation. From age six to twelve the child is in a latency period. The child shifts his or her focus from the self to social activities and making same-sex friends. The final stage is the genital stage in which heterosexual interests prevail. The way in which a person resolves conflicts between the id and the environment at each stage determines basic personality traits that last a lifetime. When a child is denied gratification or receives excess gratification at a given stage, fixation can result. This means the person's adult behavior will reflect that stage. (**Psychoanalytic approach**)

77. The superego develops in the phallic stage when the child sexually desires the opposite-sex parent. The child fears punishment from the same-sex parent which may result in repression of this conflict. This conflict is referred to as the Oedipus complex for boys and the Electra complex for girls. This conflict is resolved when the child identifies with the same-sex parent and adopts ethical standards, although the processes are not exactly the same for girls and boys. Boys are believed to fear castration, which helps them to transform the love for their mothers to an identification with their fathers. Girls are believed to have penis envy and must transform the love for their fathers into identification with their mothers. **(Psychoanalytic approach)**

78. *Neurotic anxiety* is the fear of adverse consequences that may follow if an id impulse is expressed. Freud also described two other kinds of anxiety: realistic and moral anxiety. *Realistic anxiety* refers to the ego's reaction to real danger. *Moral anxiety* is guilt or shame that results from the fear of punishment for failing to adhere to the superego's standards of morality. **(Psychoanalytic approach)**

79. Although the ego is primarily conscious, the ego has unconscious aspects such as defense mechanisms. These protect the ego from anxiety. When the ego experiences anxiety, several maneuvers can be used to relieve this discomfort. Realistic anxiety can be dealt with rationally, either by avoidance or handling the anxiety-provoking stimulus. Neurotic anxiety may be handled by an unconscious distortion of reality by defense mechanisms. Defense mechanisms, thus, are unconscious strategies used to protect the ego from anxiety. The most important defense mechanism may be *repression*, where thoughts unacceptable to the ego are pushed into the unconscious. Repression prevents awareness and keeps buried desires out of awareness. *Projection* is another defense mechanism in which people attribute to others unacceptable characteristics or desires possessed by an individual. *Displacement* is another defense mechanism where a person redirects emotional responses from a perhaps dangerous object to a safer substitute. *Reaction formation* is a defense mechanism that converts a feeling into its opposite. *Regression* means retreating to the behaviors more characteristic of an earlier developmental period. *Rationalization* involves inventing excuses for behaviors or attitudes. **(Psychoanalytic approach)**

80. Jung proposed ideas that differed greatly from those of Freud and established "analytical psychology." Jung de-emphasized the sexual nature of the libido, regarding it as a general life energy. Jung believed that we have a *collective unconscious*, which contains information from mankind's social history and positive, creative forces. Jung believed that all of us have masculine and feminine traits and that people have basic spiritual needs. Jung discussed personality traits, such as introversion-extraversion. Jung also discussed self-actualization, which he saw as the result of a balance of all personality aspects. Self-actualization means that people strive to fulfill their human potential. Jung did not focus on the past as Freud did. Jung focused on decision making and goal setting. **(Psychoanalytic approach)**

81. Adler's "individual psychology" also differed greatly from Freud's notions. Adler focused on the need to strive to overcome deficiencies, a striving for superiority. Adler thought of superiority in the sense of achieving one's potential, not in terms of competing with others. Adler believed that people find fulfillment in doing things for social benefit. **(Psychoanalytic approach)**

82. Erikson is referred to as an ego psychologist because he emphasized the development of ego identity. His eight stages of development range from infancy to mature adults. Each stage is marked by a psychosocial crisis that may have either a positive or negative resolution. **(Psychoanalytic approach)**

83. Psychoanalytic therapy tries to assist patients in removing earlier repression and facing childhood conflicts in order to reach a resolution of that conflict. Repression prevents the ego from properly developing at the individual ages. In order for the ego to fully mature, the repression must be overcome. **(Psychoanalytic approach)**

84. One of the best-known psychoanalytic technique is free association, which encourages patients to freely say whatever comes to mind, without censorship. Another technique that is used is dream analysis. Psychoanalytic theory states that normally repressed material can enter consciousness during sleep because the ego defenses are relaxed. Because this material is disturbing to us, it usually appears disguised in our dreams. Dreams must be analyzed for symbolic content that may reveal repressed desires. **(Psychoanalytic approach)**

85. Classical conditioning was originally described by Ivan Pavlov. "Conditioned" refers to the fact that a connection must be learned, while "unconditioned" refers to a connection that is innate or natural. In experiments on dogs' digestive systems, he discovered that the dog would salivate in anticipation before being fed when it saw Pavlov's assistant. He ran many experiments in order to investigate this phenomenon. A bell was rung and then the dog was fed with meat powder. After this procedure was repeated many times, the dog began salivating when it heard the bell ring. The meat powder normally elicits salivation from the dog, so the meat powder is the unconditioned stimulus (UCS) and the response of salivation to the meat powder is an unconditioned response (UCR). When the bell is paired with the neutral stimulus, it also elicits salivation. The sound of the bell is a conditioned stimulus (CS) because the dog was trained to respond to it. Salivation to the sound of the bell is the conditioned response (CR). Classical conditioning occurs when a previously neutral stimulus (bell) is paired with an unconditioned stimulus and elicits a conditioned response. Classical conditioning is learning that two stimuli are associated and responding to the conditioned stimulus. **(Learning approach)**

86. Operant conditioning began with the work of Edward Thorndike who proposed that behavior that is followed by satisfying consequences will be repeated and behavior that is followed by aversive consequences will not be repeated. This is called the law of effect. B. F. Skinner then applied this law to human behavior. Skinner believed that behavior is determined by consequences provided by the environment. Behavior is followed by a consequence that determines whether or not that behavior will occur again. The consequences that follow behavior are either reinforcements or punishment. Reinforcers will increase the likelihood that the behavior will reoccur while punishment results in the behavior being suppressed. Skinner emphasized the importance of positive reinforcement in shaping and maintaining human behavior. **(Learning approach)**

87. Modeling is a crucial component of social learning theory. Bandura proposed that we learn by watching and imitating others. Witnessing a model perform a behavior will influence our own behavior. When we see a model being reinforced for behavior, we are more likely to engage in that behavior. If we see a model being punished for a behavior, then we are less likely to engage in that behavior. **(Learning approach)**

88. Counterconditioning means that a response to a specific stimulus is eliminated when replaced by a new response in the presence of the same stimulus. Counterconditioning may help treat phobias by replacing a fear response with a non-fear response to a specific stimulus. **(Learning approach)**

89. The focus of cognitive psychology is on how people structure their experiences and how they understand them. From a cognitive perspective, the learning process is much more complex than learning theorists believe. The learner actively interprets situations with reference to prior experiences. New information must be fitted into the existing network of knowledge. Cognitive psychologists study how we acquire, store, and retrieve information and memories. **(Cognitive approach)**

90. Cognitive-behavior therapists try to alter the thought processes of clients in order to change their emotions and behavior. One major cognitive therapist, Albert Ellis, believes that maladaptive feelings and behaviors are the result of irrational beliefs. An example of an irrational belief is thinking that you

must be perfect in every way. Ellis' therapy, *rational emotive behavior therapy* (REBT), helps patients challenge beliefs and teaches them how to substitute rational thoughts. **(Cognitive approach)**

91. The humanistic approach arose largely as a reaction against psychoanalysis. Abraham Maslow was a pioneer in humanism who had a positive view of human nature. He believes that people are basically healthy and unique with a drive toward self-actualization. Humans by nature are resourceful, active, and good. Suffering is the result of a denial of this basic human goodness. **(Humanistic approach)**

92. Client-centered therapy is the best known humanistic therapeutic approach and was developed by Carl Rogers. The person seeking therapy is regarded as a client rather than a patient and is responsible for the course of his or her treatment. Therapists create conditions that help clients discover their feelings and make their own decisions. There are three conditions necessary for effective treatment in this approach: empathy, unconditional positive regard, and genuineness. Empathy is being able to take the perspective of the clients, to "walk a mile in their shoes" so to speak. It is not sympathy which involves feeling pity for a person. Empathy allows the therapist to see the world through the client's eyes. Unconditional positive regard means that the therapist accepts the client as a person worthy of dignity and respect, regardless of his or her behavior. Genuineness is communicated by the therapist who is honest and willing to share some of his or her own experiences when necessary. **(Humanistic approach)**

93. The biopsychosocial approach reflects the current view of psychopathology as the result of a complex interaction of biological, psychological, and social factors. These factors influence one another and it is this interaction that leads to behaviors. **(Humanistic approach)**

Grade Yourself

Circle the numbers of the questions you missed, then fill in the total incorrect for each topic. If you answered more than three questions incorrectly, you need to focus on that topic. (If a topic has fewer than three questions and you had at least one wrong, we suggest you study that topic also. Read your textbook or a review book, or ask your teacher for help.)

Subject: Theoretical Approaches to Abnormal Psychology

Topic	Question Numbers	Number Incorrect
Definitions	1, 2, 3, 4, 5, 6, 7, 8, 9, 10, 11, 12, 13, 14, 15, 16, 17, 18, 19, 20, 21, 22, 23, 24, 25, 26, 27, 28, 29, 30, 31, 32, 33, 34, 35, 36, 37, 38, 39	
Physiological approach	40, 41, 72, 73	
Psychoanalytic approach	42, 43, 44, 45, 46, 47, 48, 49, 50, 51, 52, 53, 54, 55, 56, 57, 58, 59, 60, 61, 62, 63, 64, 74, 75, 76, 77, 78, 79, 80, 81, 82, 83, 84	
Learning approach	65, 66, 67, 85, 86, 87, 88	
Cognitive approach	68, 69, 89, 90	
Humanistic approach	70, 71, 91, 92, 93	

Clinical Assessment and Diagnosis

3

Brief Yourself

Clinical assessment is a systematic evaluation of a person's psychological, biological and social characteristics when presenting for treatment for a psychological disorder. The clinician should at first collect information from a variety of sources. Then the clinician narrows the focus to areas that are problematic. Three concepts are important in determining the value of an assessment: *reliability*, *validity* and *standardization*. Reliability refers to measures consistency over time. Validity refers to the degree to which a measurement technique measures what it claims to measure. Standardization refers to application of norms and consistent procedures across different measurements. Clinical assessment includes several techniques including interviews, physical examination, behavioral observation and psychological tests.

Classification refers to an effort to construct categories of mental disorders and assign people's behaviors to these categories using attributes of their behavior. The first attempt at such classification was made by Emil Kraeplin. Currently, the *Diagnostic and Statistical Manual of Mental Disorders*, fourth edition (DSM-IV), is the classification system of the American Psychiatric Association used by clinicians to diagnose psychological problems. One area not covered by the DSM is the cause of psychological disorders. Beginning with the third edition of the DSM, a multiaxial diagnostic system has been used, classifying people on five separate axes. When we diagnose a person, we are labeling him or her. This label may lead to stigmatization and dehumanization of the individual. People may believe that a disorder implies that a person is bad or dangerous. That is not true. Not all mentally ill people are dangerous. Also, we may think of abnormal and normal as separate categories, when in fact they may be two ends of a continuum.

Test Yourself

Define the following terms:

1. Reliability

2. Validity

3. Standardization

4. Clinical interview

5. Mental status exam

6. Sensorium

7. Projective tests

8. MMPI

9. Rorschach inkblot test

10. Neuropsychological tests

11. DSM-IV

12. Axis I

13. Axis II

14. Axis III

15. Axis IV

16. Axis V

17. Etiology

18. Diagnosis

19. Prognosis

Questions 20–38 are true-false.

20. Validity refers to the consistency of a measure over time.

21. Reliability ensures that similar procedures are used in measurement across different situations.

22. Clinicians want to gather information about a person's family, sexual history, religious views, education and cultural concerns.

23. Affect reflects the predominant feeling of the person.

24. Mood reflects the feelings that accompany our thoughts and words.

25. Rate, continuity, and content of speech help a clinician assess cognitive functioning.

26. Observations focus on the antecedents of a behavior, the behavior itself, and the consequences of that behavior.

27. Objective tests have one advantage over projective tests: they are harder to fake.

28. There is some overlap between intelligence tests and neuropsychological tests.

29. The DSM-IV has four axes.

30. The DSM-IV lists the etiology of all disorders.

31. Axis I includes personality and developmental disorders.

32. Axis II includes all diagnostic categories.

33. Axis III indicates physical illnesses which may affect the client.

34. Axis IV reflects global adaptive functioning.

35. Axis V encompasses psychosocial and environmental problems faced by the client.

36. Etiology refers to the prognosis of a disorder.

37. All mentally ill people are dangerous.

38. Labeling is dehumanizing.

39. Describe the three concepts needed to understand assessment.

40. What is a clinical interview?

41. Describe the mental status exam.

42. What is meant by behavioral assessment?

43. What does the clinician try to observe?

44. What are psychological tests?

45. Describe projective tests.

46. Are objective tests more reliable?

47. Do clinicians use intelligence tests also?

48. What are neuropsychological tests?

49. Discuss the classification of mental disorders.

50. What is the DSM-IV?

51. How does the DSM-IV classify mental disorders?

52. What issues are important when discussing diagnosis of psychological disorders?

53. What myths do people believe in regard to people with psychological disorders?

 # Check Yourself

1. Reliability refers to the consistency of a measure over time. (**Assessment concepts**)

2. Validity refers to the fact that an instrument or test measures what it claims to measure. (**Assessment concepts**)

3. Standardization ensures that similar procedures are used in measurement across different situations. (**Assessment concepts**)

4. The clinical interview is used by most mental health professionals to gather information on current and past behaviors and feelings. (**Clinical interviews**)

5. The mental status exam is usually given during a clinical interview and is an evaluation of the clients' judgment, temporal orientation, and emotional state. This exam covers five categories: physical appearance, thought processes, emotions, intellectual functioning and sensorium. (**Clinical interviews**)

6. Sensorium refers to a general awareness of one's environment. (**Clinical interviews**)

7. Projective tests present a person with ambiguous stimuli to respond to. It is believed that a person's response reflects underlying psychological processes and will reveal unconscious conflicts. (**Psychological tests**)

8. The most widely used personality inventory in the United States is the Minnesota Multiphasic Personality Inventory (MMPI). (**Psychological tests**)

9. The most widely used projective tests contains a series of 10 cards with inkblots on them, the Rorschach inkblot test. (**Psychological tests**)

10. Neuropsychological tests assess brain and nervous system functioning by testing performance on certain tasks. (**Neuropsychological tests**)

11. DSM-IV is the current diagnostic system used to classify mental disorders. (**Classification**)

12. Axis I includes all diagnostic categories except personality and developmental disorders. (**Classification**)

13. Axis II categorizes personality and developmental disorders. (**Classification**)

14. Axis III indicates any physical illness which may affect a psychological disorder. (**Classification**)

15. Axis IV indicates the psychosocial and environmental problems that may affect the psychological disorder. (**Classification**)

16. Axis V categorizes the global adaptive functioning of a client. (**Classification**)

17. Etiology refers to the cause of a disorder. (**Classification**)

18. Diagnosis is the classification of a particular group of symptoms as a particular disorder. (**Diagnostic issues**)

19. Prognosis refers to the expected outcome of a disorder or illness. (**Diagnostic issues**)

20. **False.** *Reliability* refers to the consistency of a measure over time. (**Assessment concepts**)

21. **False.** *Standardization* ensures that similar procedures are used in measurement across different situations. (**Assessment concepts**)

22. **True.** Clinicians want to gather information about a person's family, sexual history, religious views, education and cultural concerns. (**Clinical interviews**)

23. **False.** *Mood* reflects the predominant feeling of the person. (**Clinical interviews**)

24. **False.** *Affect* reflects the feelings that accompany our thoughts and words. (**Clinical interviews**)

25. **True.** Rate, continuity, and content of speech help a clinician assess cognitive functioning. (**Clinical interviews**)

26. **True.** Observations focus on the antecedents of a behavior, the behavior itself, and the consequences of that behavior. (**Behavioral observations**)

27. **False.** *Projective tests* have one advantage over objective tests: they are harder to fake. (**Psychological tests**)

28. **True.** There is some overlap between intelligence tests and neuropsychological tests. (**Neuropsychological tests**)

29. **False.** The DSM-IV has *five* axes. (**Classification**)

30. **False.** The DSM-IV *does not* list the etiology of all disorders. (**Classification**)

31. **False.** Axis I *does not* include personality and developmental disorders. (**Classification**)

32. **False.** Axis II *does not* includes all diagnostic categories. (**Classification**)

33. **True.** Axis III indicates physical illnesses which may affect the client. (**Classification**)

34. **False.** Axis *V* reflects global adaptive functioning. (**Classification**)

35. **False.** Axis *IV* encompasses psychosocial and environmental problems faced by the client. (**Classification**)

36. **False.** Etiology refers to the *cause* of a disorder. (**Classification**)

37. **False.** *Not* all mentally ill people are dangerous. (**Diagnostic issues**)

38. **True.** Labeling is dehumanizing. (**Diagnostic issues**)

39. The first is reliability which refers to the consistency of a measure over time. Consistency in diagnosis is important. You would expect someone who went to several clinicians presenting the same symptoms to get the same diagnosis. The degree to which this is true is called reliability. Validity is important also. Measures should measure what they say they measure, otherwise we have no idea what we are measuring. Standardization ensures that similar procedures are used in measurement across different situations. There should be standard procedures for administering a test or measure, for scoring it and interpreting it. Also, these measures are often given to large groups to get a reference point or standard against which to compare a persons performance. (**Assessment concepts**)

40. The clinical interview is used by most mental health professionals to gather information on current and past behaviors and feelings. Also, it is useful to gather information about a person's life history. Clinicians focus on the present problem and try to get more information about it. Clinicians also want to get information about a person's family, sexual history, religious views, education and cultural concerns. One of the first things done in a clinical interview is the mental status exam. (**Clinical interviews**)

41. A mental status exam is usually given during a clinical interview and is an evaluation of the clients' judgment, temporal orientation, and emotional state. This exam covers five categories: physical appearance, thought processes, emotions, intellectual functioning and sensorium. Physical appearance means that the clinician notices the way a person is dressed, posture, facial expressions and overt behaviors. When talking to a client, the clinician can get a good idea of a person's thought processes. Rate, continuity, and content of speech help a clinician assess cognitive functioning. The clinician can also detect if any delusions or hallucinations are present. Determining mood or emotion is an important part of this exam. Mood reflects the predominant feeling of the person. Affect reflects the feelings that accompany our thoughts and words. Clinicians also try to roughly estimate a person's intellectual functioning by talking to them. One can measure intellectual functioning by vocabulary, use of metaphors and abstractions, and memory. Sensorium refers to a general awareness of one's environment. Sensorium can be measured by assessing people's self, time and place orientation. Do they know who they are? Do they know where they are? Do they know what day and time it is? (**Clinical interviews**)

42. Behavioral assessment involves formally assessing a person's thoughts, feelings and behavior in specific contexts. This information is used to try to explain why the individual is having problems. Sometimes interviews are not as useful as they could be because the client is a young child, is withholding information, or has limited verbal skills. Behavioral assessment identifies target behaviors which are observed in order to determine what influences these behaviors. If actually going to a person's home, work or school is not feasible, an analogous situation may be set up to see how the person behaves. (**Behavioral observations**)

43. Observations focus on the antecedents of a behavior, the behavior itself, and the consequences of that behavior. Observation can be informal, as in observing and making mental notes, or more formal or structured, such as using rating scales to measure behaviors. (**Behavioral observations**)

44. Psychological tests are often used to assess psychological disorders and have good reliability and validity. There are two types of psychological tests: projective and objective tests. (**Psychological tests**)

45. Projective tests present a person with ambiguous stimuli to respond to. It is believed that a person's response reflects underlying psychological processes and will reveal unconscious conflicts. People are thought to "project" their own personality and fears onto the test. The most widely used projective tests contains a series of 10 cards with inkblots on them, the Rorschach inkblot test. The person is shown a card and asked to tell the clinician what they see. Another widely used test, the thematic apperception

test (TAT), contains cards with pictures on them and the client is asked to make up a story to go along with the picture. Projective tests have one advantage over objective tests: they are harder to fake because there is no right or wrong answer. Projective tests are commonly used; however, they lack the reliability and validity of objective instruments. They are useful in some situations but not as a sole diagnostic tool. **(Psychological tests)**

46. Yes, objective tests typically have greater reliability and validity than a projective measure. Objective tests are usually based on empirical data rather than theory. Many objective tests try to measure aspects of one's personality. The most widely used personality inventory in the United States is the *Minnesota Multiphasic Personality Inventory*, second edition (MMPI-2). The MMPI-2 contains a series of statements to which a person responds true or false. The administration, scoring and norms have been standardized. **(Psychological tests)**

47. Sometimes. An IQ score, which is a score on an intelligence test, predicts academic performance. There is much debate about the nature of intelligence and it is important to remember that IQ tests do not necessarily measure intelligence. IQ tests tap into various cognitive tasks, but do these tasks represent intelligence? Some theorists believe that intelligence is much more and includes adaptability to the environment and generation of new ideas. Neither of these are measured by IQ tests. **(Psychological tests)**

48. Neuropsychological tests assess brain and nervous system functioning by testing performance on certain tasks. Individuals are tested on their language abilities, attention, memory, motor skills, perceptual skills, and learning. Brain dysfunction is assessed by observing a person's ability to perform certain tasks. Some tests allow the clinician to determine the exact location of the dysfunction. There is some overlap between intelligence tests and neuropsychological tests. These tests tend to be reliable and valid. However, these tests require many hours to administer and are not used unless brain damage is suspected. **(Neuropsychological tests)**

49. Classification refers to an effort to construct categories of mental disorders and assign people's behaviors to these categories using attributes of his or her behavior. The first attempt at such classification was made by Emil Kraeplin. He assumed that each disorder had a physiological cause and that each disorder was distinct. Classifications aid in categorizing these disorders and communicating about these disorders. Today the *Diagnostic and Statistical Manual of Mental Disorders*, fourth edition (DSM-IV), which is based on empirical research, is used by psychiatrists and psychologists to make diagnoses. This manual has evolved since its first edition in the 1952. Each revision attempted to increase the reliability, validity and utility of the DSM. **(Classification)**

50. *The Diagnostic and Statistical Manual of Mental Disorders* (1994), fourth edition (DSM-IV), is the classification system of the American Psychiatric Association. It is used by clinicians to diagnose psychological problems. One area not covered by the DSM is etiology, or the causes, of psychological disorders. **(Classification)**

51. Beginning with the third edition of the DSM, a multiaxial diagnostic system has been used. This means that each person presenting for diagnosis is classified on five separate dimensions. This forces the clinician to consider more than just symptomatology. Axis I includes all diagnostic categories except personality and developmental disorders, which are categorized on Axis II. These first two axes represent the classification of abnormal behavior according to symptoms. Axis III indicates physical illnesses which may affect the psychological disorder. Axis IV indicates the psychosocial and environmental problems that may affect the psychological disorder. Such problems include support group problems (e.g., family disruption), environmental problems (e.g., death of a friend), educational problems (e.g., illiteracy), occupational problems (e.g., unemployment), housing problems (e.g.,

homelessness), economic problems (poverty), difficulty accessing health care (inadequate health insurance), and problems with the criminal justice system (e.g., incarceration). Axis V indicates the person's global functioning. This category includes social, occupational, and leisure functioning. **(Classification)**

52. When we diagnose a person, we are attaching a label to his or her behavior. This label may lead to stigmatization of the individual. People may treat this person differently because of this label and their preconceived ideas about the mentally ill. Also, when we use a label we may be dehumanizing that individual. Our focus is on the disorder, not the person. Also, we place all responsibility for the disorder on an individual when making a diagnosis. **(Diagnostic issues)**

53. People may believe that a disorder implies that a person is bad or dangerous. That is not true. Not all mentally ill people are dangerous. We may believe that because of the media's sensationalizing events. We are shown on TV mentally disturbed people holding hostages; we are shown the aftermath of mass killings also. What we are shown are extreme examples of pathology. These are not typical. Most people with psychological disorders are not dangerous. Also, we may think of abnormal and normal as separate categories, when in fact they may be two sides of one coin. **(Diagnostic issues)**

Grade Yourself

Circle the numbers of the questions you missed, then fill in the total incorrect for each topic. If you answered more than three questions incorrectly, you need to focus on that topic. (If a topic has fewer than three questions and you had at least one wrong, we suggest you study that topic also. Read your textbook or a review book, or ask your teacher for help.)

Subject: Clinical Assessment and Diagnosis

Topic	Question Numbers	Number Incorrect
Assessment concepts	1, 2, 3	
Clinical interviews	4, 5, 6, 22, 23, 24, 25, 40, 41	
Psychological tests	7, 8, 9, 27, 44, 45, 46, 47	
Neuropsychological tests	10, 28, 48	
Classification	11, 12, 13, 14, 15, 16, 17, 29, 30, 31, 32, 33, 34, 35, 36, 49, 50, 51	
Diagnostic issues	18, 19, 37, 38, 52, 53	
Assessment concepts	20, 21, 39	
Behavioral observations	26, 42, 43	

Research Methods in Experimental Psychology

4

Brief Yourself

Science demands specific techniques for collecting and interpreting data in order to build a body of knowledge. Scientific statements must be testable, subject to falsification, and based on reliable observations; and constructs must be linked to measurable outcomes. Psychology involves the study of many behaviors and at times links these behaviors to underlying cognitive or affective processes such as thoughts, emotions, attitudes, beliefs, etc. Yet, these constructs are always linked to events that are measurable. Scientists use many methods to gather and interpret data, such as *epidemiological methods*; *case studies*; and *correlational*, *experimental*, and *single-subject research*, all of which have advantages and disadvantages. The choice of a research method depends upon the research question being asked. Epidemiological research examines the prevalence of various disorders and risk factors that may be lead to a higher likelihood of having a disorder. Case studies are very important in psychopathology. They allow an in-depth examination of rare phenomena and generate hypotheses used in other types of controlled research. Correlational research is very important in psychopathology due to the classificatory nature of disorders. This method allows us to determine which variables co-occur or are related. However, this method is limited because of its inability to make cause-effect statements. The only research method that allows us to make cause-effect conclusions is the experiment. The experiment occurs under controlled conditions in which one variable is manipulated in order to determine its effect on another variable. However, even this method may be subject to bias and limitations.

Test Yourself

Define the terms in questions 1–18.

1. Theory

2. Epidemiology

3. Prevalence

4. Incidence

5. Risk factor

6. Correlational method

7. Correlation coefficient

8. Statistical significance

9. Hypothesis

10. Independent variable

11. Dependent variable

12. Control group

13. Experimental group

14. Internal validity

15. External validity

16. Random assignment

17. Double blind

18. ABAB design

Questions 19– 44 are true-false.

19. Scientific statements must be testable.

20. Scientific statements are based on reliable inferences.

21. Scientific statements are linked to measurable outcomes.

22. Falsifiability refers to subjecting these propositions to systematic examination.

23. Psychopathology uses only one method to study abnormal behavior, the case study.

24. In epidemiological studies data are collected regarding the rates of disease and other variables associated with this disease in a large sample.

25. Prevalence refers to the number of new cases of a disorder that occur in a specific time period, like a year.

26. Incidence refers to the proportion of a population that has a disorder at a specific point in time or during a specific period of time.

27. A risk factor is a condition that, if present, increases the probability of developing a disorder.

28. Case-study data has demonstrated that depression is more prevalent in women than men.

29. Case studies lack the control and objectivity of experiments.

30. Correlational methods are most useful in clinical settings where one person is being examined.

31. The correlational method tells us whether a relationship exists between two or more variables.

32. The correlation coefficient is r, which ranges from 0 to 1.

33. The correlation coefficient has both magnitude and direction.

34. When $r = 1$, there is no relationship between the two variables.

35. Direction refers to the strength of the relationship, indicated by the sign of r.

36. A positive r means that there is an inverse relationship between the two variables: as one variable increases, the other variable decreases.

37. Statistical significance tells us the probability that a relationship occurred by chance.

38. A correlation is considered statistically significant if the likelihood that the finding is due to chance is 5 or more in 100.

39. The correlational method allows us to draw cause-effect conclusions.

40. In an experiment, one variable is manipulated under controlled conditions, in order to see how it affects another variable.

41. Random assignment of subjects means that some subjects have more chance of being in the experimental group.

42. The control group of subjects experiences the manipulation of the independent variable.

43. In an experiment, the independent variable is manipulated.

44. The single subject design is usually called an ABAB or reversal design.

45. What conditions are demanded by a scientific approach?

46. Discuss testability and falsifiability.

47. Discuss the concept of theory and its role in the scientific approach.

48. Which research methods are used to study abnormal behavior?

49. Discuss epidemiological research and the concepts of prevalence, incidence and risk factors.

50. Give some examples of what we have learned about psychopathology using epidemiological research.

51. What is a case study?

52. How have case studies been used?

53. What are the limitations of the case-study approach?

54. What is the major advantage of the case-study approach?

55. What is the correlational method?

56. Discuss the correlation coefficient and its properties.

57. Which of the following correlation coefficients reflects a stronger relationship between variables: $r = -.80$ or $r = +.20$?

58. What is meant by statistical significance?

59. What are some problems with the correlational method?

60. What is an experiment?

61. Discuss the basic features of an experiment.

62. What is meant by "double blind"?

63. Discuss the single-subject experimental design.

64. What are some limitations of the single-subject design?

65. Discuss the multiple baseline design.

 # Check Yourself

1. A theory is a set of propositions or statements that attempt to explain a phenomenon. (**Scientific methods**)

2. Epidemiology involves the study of the frequency with which an illness or disease occurs in a population and how it is distributed in that population. (**Epidemiological research**)

3. Prevalence refers to the proportion of a population that has a disorder at a specific point in time or during a specific period of time. (**Epidemiological research**)

4. Incidence refers to the number of new cases of a disorder that occur in a specific time period, like a year. (**Epidemiological research**)

5. A risk factor is a condition that, if present, increases the probability of developing a disorder. (**Epidemiological research**)

6. The correlational method establishes whether a relationship exists between two or more variables. (**Correlational research**)

7. The measure of this relationship is the correlation coefficient *r*, which ranges from 0 to 1. This correlation coefficient has both magnitude and direction. (**Correlational research**)

8. Statistical significance tells us the probability that a relationship occurred by chance. (**Correlational research**)

9. A hypothesis is a statement about how constructs may be related causally. (**Experimental studies**)

10. The independent variable is the variable that is manipulated in an experiment. (**Experimental studies**)

11. The dependent variable is the variable that is measured in an experiment. (**Experimental studies**)

12. The control group receives no manipulation of the independent variable. (**Experimental studies**)

13. The experimental group of subjects experiences the manipulation of the independent variable. (**Experimental studies**)

14. Research in which the effects can be attributed to the manipulation of the independent variable is said to be internally valid. (**Experimental studies**)

15. External validity refers to the generalizability of the results of a study to other samples or populations. (**Experimental studies**)

16. By randomly assigning subjects, each subject has an equal chance of being in either the control or experimental group. This is important because both groups must be as similar as possible in order to claim that any group differences that occur in the experiment are due to the independent variable. (**Experimental studies**)

17. Double blind is a technique in which neither the experimenter nor the subjects know who is in the control and experimental groups, helping eliminate experimenter and subject bias. (**Experimental studies**)

18. The ABAB design is a single-subject experimental design which involves measures of behavior at four points in time, baseline (A), introduction of treatment (B), return to baseline conditions (A) and reintroduction of treatment (B). (**Experimental studies**)

19. **True.** Scientific statements must be testable. (**Scientific methods**)

20. **False.** Scientific statements are based on reliable *observations*. (**Scientific methods**)

21. **True.** Scientific statements are linked to measurable outcomes. (**Scientific methods**)

22. **False.** *Testability* refers to subjecting these propositions to systematic examination. (**Scientific methods**)

23. **False.** Psychopathology uses *many* methods to study abnormal behavior, including *epidemiological, case-study, correlational* and *experimental methods.* (**Scientific methods**)

24. **True.** In epidemiological studies data are collected regarding the rates of disease and other variables associated with this disease in a large sample. **(Epidemiological research)**

25. **False.** Prevalence refers to the proportion of a population that has a disorder at a specific point in time or during a specific period of time. **(Epidemiological research)**

26. **False.** Incidence refers to the number of new cases of a disorder that occur in a specific time period. **(Epidemiological research)**

27. **True.** A risk factor is a condition that, if present, increases the probability of developing a disorder. **(Epidemiological research)**

28. **False.** *Epidemiological* data have demonstrated that depression is more prevalent in women than men. **(Epidemiological research)**

29. **True.** Case studies lack the control and objectivity of experiments. **(Case study)**

30. **False.** *Case studies* are most useful in clinical settings where one person is being examined. **(Case study)**

31. **True.** The correlational method tells us whether a relationship exists between two or more variables. **(Correlational research)**

32. **False.** The correlation coefficient *r* ranges from 0 to 1. **(Correlational research)**

33. **True.** The correlation coefficient has both magnitude and direction. **(Correlational research)**

34. **False.** When *r=0*, there is no relationship between the two variables. **(Correlational research)**

35. **False.** *Magnitude* refers to the strength of the relationship, indicated by the *numerical value* of *r*. **(Correlational research)**

36. **False.** A *negative r* means that there is an inverse relationship between the two variables: as one variable increases, the other variable decreases. **(Correlational research)**

37. **True.** Statistical significance tells us the probability that a relationship occurred by chance. **(Correlational research)**

38. **False.** A correlation is considered statistically significant if the likelihood that the finding is due to chance is 5 or *less* in 100. **(Correlational research)**

39. **False.** The correlational method *does not allow* us to draw cause-effect conclusions. **(Correlational research)**

40. **True.** In an experiment, one variable is manipulated, under controlled conditions, in order to see how it affects another variable. **(Experimental studies)**

41. **False.** Random assignment of subjects means that *all subjects have equal* chances of being in the experimental group *or control group*. **(Experimental studies)**

42. **False.** The *experimental* group of subjects experiences the manipulation of the independent variable. **(Experimental studies)**

43. **True.** In an experiment, the independent variable is manipulated. **(Experimental studies)**

44. **True**. The single-subject design is usually called an ABAB or reversal design. **(Experimental studies)**

45. Scientific statements must be testable, subject to falsification, and based on reliable observations; and constructs must be linked to measurable events or outcomes. **(Scientific methods)**

46. Testability demands that scientific propositions be stated clearly and precisely. This is a necessary precondition for testability. Testability refers to subjecting these propositions to systematic examination. All hypotheses, propositions, and claims must be examined in a systematic manner, regardless of the plausibility of these claims. These statements must be publicly testable and be subject to being disapproved. Falsifiability refers to demonstrating that a proposition or hypothesis is wrong. **(Scientific methods)**

47. A theory is a set of propositions or statements that attempt to explain a phenomenon. Science tries to advance theories that will shed light on the information with which it deals, in order to better understand many different kinds of phenomena. Empirical research allows us to test the adequacy of such theories. Scientists may infer unobservable processes from observable data in generating theories or may use theories to account for previously observed relationships. **(Scientific methods)**

48. Psychopathology uses many methods to study abnormal behavior, including epidemiological, case-study, correlational and experimental methods. **(Scientific methods)**

49. Epidemiology involves the study of the frequency with which an illness or disease occurs in a population and how it is distributed in that population. Data are collected regarding the rates of disease and other variables associated with this disease in a large sample. Prevalence refers to the proportion of a population that has a disorder at a specific point in time or during a specific period of time. Incidence refers to the number of new cases of a disorder that occur in a specific time period, like a year. A risk factor is a condition that, if present, increases the probability of developing a disorder. **(Epidemiological research)**

50. Epidemiological data have demonstrated that depression is more prevalent in women than men and that schizophrenia is most prevalent in the lowest socioeconomic class. **(Epidemiological research)**

51. In a case study, historical and biographical information about the person being studied is collected by a clinician. This approach involves an in-depth study of this person and his or her disorder, so as much information as possible is gathered. Information collected includes family history, medical history, educational background, employment history, marital history, and any information about the person's personality, development, adjustment and current functioning. This information is gathered from the individual and other sources. **(Case study)**

52. Case studies have been used to provide an in-depth description of rare occurrences, allow examination of assumed universal aspects of a theory and are useful in generating hypotheses that can be tested by other more controlled research methods. **(Case study)**

53. Case studies lack the control and objectivity of experiments and only provide information about one particular case, thereby limiting the generalizability of results. Also, the validity of the information gathered is sometimes questionable. The case-study method does not allow one to make cause-effect conclusions as an experiment would. **(Case study)**

54. The case study is most useful in clinical settings where one person is being examined. It provides valuable information on the psychological composition of this person and his or her behavior. **(Case study)**

55. The correlational method establishes whether a relationship exists between two or more variables. This method can be used in epidemiological or psychological research. **(Correlational research)**

56. Data are gathered on subjects on at least two variables. Then we can determine the exact nature of the relationship between these two variables. The measure of this relationship is the correlation coefficient r, which ranges from 0 to 1. This correlation coefficient has both magnitude and direction. Magnitude refers to the strength of the relationship and is indicated by the numerical value of r. The higher the number, the greater the relationship. When $r=0$, there is no relationship between the two variables. When $r=1$, there is a perfect relationship between the two variables. The direction of the correlation is determined by the sign of r. A positive r means that there is a positive relationship between the two variables: as one variable increases or decreases, the other variable does likewise. A negative r means that there is an inverse relationship between the two variables: as one variable increases, the other variable decreases. **(Correlational research)**

57. The strength of a correlationis indicated by the number and the sign tells us the direction of the relationship. The stronger relationship is $r = -.80$ because the number (80) is greater than the other correlation (20). Don't let the negative sign confuse you. The only aspect one needs to look at to determine the strength of a relationship is the number. The sign tells us about direction; therefore the $-.80$ means that the two variables are inversely related (one is increasing while the other is decreasing) and the 20 tells us there is a positive relationship (both variables are increasing or decreasing). **(Correlational research)**

58. Statistical significance tells us the probability that a relationship occurred by chance. If the study was conducted again, we would be unlikely to get the same results if our results were due to chance. Traditionally, a correlation is considered statistically significant if the likelihood that the finding is due to chance is 5 or less in 100. Significance is indicated by the probability level, written as p.05. This means that there is a 5 out of 100 probability that our results were due to chance. This level or lower is acceptable in psychological research. Therefore, a probability level of .05, .01, .001, or .0001 is acceptable. **(Correlational research)**

59. This method does not allow us to draw cause-effect conclusions. It only lets us state whether a relationship exists, how strong the relationship is and the direction of the relationship. When two variables are correlated, we know they are related but we do not know which variable might be cause and which might be effect. Or it may be that another variable is causing both of the variables being studied, referred to as the "third variable problem." **(Correlational research)**

60. The experiment is the only way to determine causal relationships. In an experiment one variable is manipulated, under controlled conditions, in order to see how it effects another variable. **(Experimental studies)**

61. The researcher begins with a hypothesis, which is a statement about how constructs may be related causally. The researcher chooses which variable will be manipulated, the independent variable, and which variable will be measured, the dependent variable. Subjects are chosen to participate in the experiment. Subjects may be assigned to one of two groups. Subjects are assigned randomly, meaning that each subject has an equal chance of being in either group. This random assignment should equal out any differences that may exist between subjects prior to the experiment, thus eliminating any bias introduced by subject differences in the two groups. The experimental group of subjects experiences the

manipulation of the independent variable, while the control group receives no manipulation. The control group is necessary if we want to attribute the effects to the manipulation of the independent variable. One group receives the manipulation and one does not. Therefore, we would expect to see differences on the dependent variable between the control group and the experimental group. **(Experimental studies)**

62. In order to avoid biases introduced by either experimenters or subjects, researchers may use a double blind procedure. This involves making sure that neither the person performing the study nor the subjects know which groups the subjects are in. Neither the experimenter nor the subject know if that subject is in the control or experimental group. This assures that any results obtained will not be influenced by the experimenter's expectations or the subject's expectations or beliefs. **(Experimental studies)**

63. The single-subject design is usually called an ABAB or reversal design. This design involves measuring a single aspect of the subject's behavior during given time periods. The behavior is measured at baseline (A) prior to experimental study, during a period in which a treatment or manipulation is introduced (B), during a reinstatement of the baseline conditions (A) which usually means withdrawal of the treatment, and last during a reintroduction of the treatment (B). If the behavior is changed by the manipulation and returns to its original state when the manipulation is withdrawn and changes again with the reintroduction of the treatment, then there can be little doubt that the treatment caused the behavior change. **(Experimental studies)**

64. There is no control group to act as a check on the subject. There is only one subject, not many, which limits the generalizability, or external validity, of the research. **(Experimental studies)**

65. In the multiple baseline design, the researcher begins treatment at different points in time, across different settings, behaviors, or people. This design helps rule out alternative explanations for behaviors, which increases the validity of the study. This design may also improve the generalizability of results by having multiple subjects, which can act as controls, instead of using a single subject. **(Experimental studies)**

Grade Yourself

Circle the numbers of the questions you missed, then fill in the total incorrect for each topic. If you answered more than three questions incorrectly, you need to focus on that topic. (If a topic has fewer than three questions and you had at least one wrong, we suggest you study that topic also. Read your textbook or a review book, or ask your teacher for help.)

Subject: Research Methods in Experimental Psychology

Topic	Question Numbers	Number Incorrect
Scientific methods	1, 19, 20, 21, 22, 23, 45, 46, 47, 48	
Epidemiological research	2, 3, 4, 5, 24, 25, 26, 27, 28, 49, 50	
Correlational research	6, 7, 8, 31, 32, 33, 34, 35, 36, 37, 38, 39, 55, 56, 57, 58, 59	
Experimental studies	9, 10, 11, 12, 13, 14, 15, 16, 17, 18, 40, 41, 42, 43, 44, 60, 61, 62, 63, 64, 65	
Case study	29, 30, 51, 52, 53, 54	

Disorders of Childhood and Adolescence

Brief Yourself

Differentiating childhood disorders from adult disorders is mostly for ease of classification rather than to imply a clear-cut distinction between the two. Childhood is an important period of growth and development for the brain as well as the rest of the body. Changes occur in social, emotional, physical, and cognitive development. A disruption of these developmental changes may disrupt the development of later skills due to the sequential nature of development.

Most people with these childhood disorders are diagnosed during childhood or adolescence; however, there are some who are not diagnosed until adulthood. In an evaluation of a child or adolescent, a clinician should refer to disorders in this and other chapters. Disorders discussed in this chapter include *attention deficit* and *disruptive behavior disorders*, *feeding or eating disorders* of infancy and childhood, *tic disorders*, and *elimination disorders*. Other disorders that may be considered as childhood disorders but involve impaired development, such as mental retardation, learning disorders, motor skills disorders, communication disorders and pervasive developmental disorders, are discussed in chapter 6.

Attention deficit-hyperactivity disorder and its subtypes are characterized by inattention and hyperactivity or impulsivity. Disruptive behavior disorders include conduct disorder and oppositional defiant disorder. Conduct disorders are characterized by behavior that violates the rights of others or age-appropriate social norms. The oppositional defiant disorder is characterized by a pattern of negative, hostile and defiant behavior. Feeding and eating disorders of childhood and infancy are characterized by persistent disturbances in feeding and eating. These disorders include pica, rumination and feeding disorder of infancy. Tic disorders are characterized by vocal and or motor tics. These disorders include Tourette's disorder, chronic motor or vocal tic disorder, and transient tic disorder. Elimination disorders include encopresis and enuresis. Encopresis involves the repeated elimination of feces in inappropriate places while enuresis involves the voiding of urine in inappropriate places.

Test Yourself

Define the terms in questions 1–7.

1. Attention deficit-hyperactivity disorder

2. Disruptive behavior disorders

3. Conduct disorder

4. Oppositional defiant disorder

5. Elimination disorders

6. Encopresis

7. Enuresis

Questions 8–14 are true-false.

8. Symptoms of hyperactivity or implusivity must occur prior to age 7 for a diagnosis of attention deficit-hyperactivity disorder to be made.

9. One symptom of inattention that is characteristic of attention deficit-hyperactivity disorder is losing things necessary for tasks.

10. One symptom of hyperactivity that is characteristic of attention deficit-hyperactivity disorder is talking excessively.

11. A symptom of impulsivity that is characteristic of attention deficit-hyperactivity disorder is interrupting other people.

12. A main sympton of oppositional defiant disorder is of recurrent behaviors which violate the rights of others or age-appropriate social rules.

13. A primary symptom of conduct disorder is of repeated negative, antagonistic, disobedient and hostile behaviors toward authority figures that endure for at least 6 months.

14. Children with conduct disorder may be physically cruel to people and/or animals.

15. What is attention deficit-hyperactivity disorder?

16. What is meant by "inattention"?

17. What is meant by "hyperactivity"?

18. What is meant by "impulsivity"?

19. What causes ADHD?

20. How is ADHD treated?

21. What is conduct disorder?

22. What are the two types of conduct disorder?

23. What causes conduct disorder?

24. How is conduct disorder treated?

25. What is oppositional defiant disorder?

26. What are the elimination disorders?

27. What is encopresis?

28. What are the main symptoms of enuresis?

Check Yourself

1. Attention deficit-hyperactivity disorder refers to a enduring pattern of inattention and/or hyperactivity/impulsivity that is more frequent and severe than usually seen in children at similar developmental levels. (**Attention deficit disorder**)

2. Disruptive behavior disorders include both conduct disorder and oppositional defiant disorder. These disorders are marked by behavior that impinges on the rights of others and is negativistic and hostile and defies authority. (**Disruptive disorders**)

3. Conduct disorders are typified by behavior that violates the rights of others or age-appropriate social norms. The oppositional defiant disorder is characterized by a pattern of negative, hostile and defiant behavior. (**Disruptive disorders**)

4. The oppositional defiant disorder is characterized by a pattern of negative, hostile and defiant behavior. (**Disruptive disorders**)

5. Elimination disorders involve the repeated voiding of feces or urine in inappropriate locations. (**Elimination disorders**)

6. Encopresis is an elimination disorder that involves the repeated elimination of feces in inappropriate places. (**Elimination disorders**)

7. Enuresis is an elimination disorder that involves the voiding of urine in inappropriate places. (**Elimination disorders**)

8. **True.** Symptoms of hyperactivity or implusivity must occur prior to age 7 for a diagnosis of attention deficit-hyperactivity disorder to be made. (**Attention deficit disorder**)

9. **True.** One symptom of inattention that is characteristic of attention deficit-hyperactivity disorder is losing things necessary for tasks. (**Attention deficit disorder**)

10. **True.** One symptom of hyperactivity that is characteristic of attention deficit-hyperactivity disorder is talking excessively. (**Attention deficit disorder**)

11. **True.** A symptom of impulsivity that is characteristic of attention deficit-hyperactivity disorder is interrupting other people. (**Attention deficit disorder**)

12. **False.** Conduct disorders' main feature is of repeated and continual behaviors which violate the rights of others or age-appropriate social rules. (**Disruptive disorders**)

13. **False.** Oppositional defiant disorders' main feature is of recurrent negative, antagonistic, disobedient and hostile behaviors toward authority figures that endure for at least 6 months. (**Disruptive disorders**)

14. **True.** Children with conduct disorder may be physically cruel to people and/or animals. (**Disruptive disorders**)

15. Attention deficit-hyperactivity disorder (ADHD) is a developmental disorder which is characterized by disruptive behavior in the form of inattention, hyperactivity or impulsivity. These behaviors disrupt academic and social functioning. These behaviors typically occur prior to age 7 and last for at least six

months. ADHD is fairly common, with boys being four times as likely to be diagnosed with ADHD than girls. These children continue to have problems in adolescence such as impulsiveness, inattention and family discord. Children with ADHD seem to improve as they get older, usually between ages 16 and 21. Children who also have a conduct disorder are less likely to improve as they get older. (**Attention deficit disorder**)

16. Inattention means that the child may not pay attention to details, be careless, have trouble concentrating, be easily distracted and not complete tasks. (**Attention deficit disorder**)

17. Hyperactivity refers to excessive activity that occurs in inappropriate situations such as not sitting still, running or climbing, and talking too much. (**Attention deficit disorder**)

18. Impulsivity refers to blurting out answers too quickly, trouble taking turns, and interrupting others. (**Attention deficit disorder**)

19. Some of the symptoms of inattention suggest some involvement of the central nervous system. However, research on neurological deficits in ADHD children has been inconclusive. Some researchers believe that certain foods or food additives may result in hyperactivity, such as sugar. Controlled studies of this hypothesis have shown that food additives have little effect on hyperactivity. There may also be family influences; however, it is difficult to separate genetic influences from environmental influences. (**Attention deficit disorder**)

20. Most children with ADHD are treated with drug therapy such as stimulants which increase attention. Almost three-fourths of children with ADHD who are treated with stimulants respond positively to this treatment. The effect of these drugs only last as long as the drug is taken; there are no long-term improvements. Some behavioral therapies, such as self-instruction, modeling, or parent training programs have been just as effective as drug therapy. (**Attention deficit disorder**)

21. Conduct disorders involve antisocial behaviors that violate the rights of other people. This behavior must recur and be persistent (last for at least 6 months) in order to be diagnosed as having a conduct disorder. Some of the behaviors seen in this disorder include cruelty to animals and people, fighting, arson, assault, rape, truancy, destroying property, lying and cheating. This disorder is much more likely to be diagnosed in males than females (4 to 5 times more likely). Sometimes this disorder is preceded by oppositional defiant disorder or ADHD. The prognosis is poor for conduct-disordered children. Many of these children become involved with alcohol, drugs, criminal activity or sexually aggressive behaviors. Females tend to have a better prognosis than males. (**Disruptive disorders**)

22. The types of conduct disorder are distinguished by their age of onset. The childhood-onset type begins prior to age 10. This means that the types of behaviors that describe this disorder occur before age 10. Most children with this type are male, behave aggressively and had oppositional defiant disorder. These children are more likely to go on to develop the antisocial personality disorder in adulthood. The other type of conduct disorder is the adolescent-onset type, in which the behaviors occur after age 10. (**Disruptive disorders**)

23. Genetic factors may play a role in the development of conduct disorders. Boys with conduct disorders tend to be more likely have antisocial parents. Studies by Mednick support the contention that there may be a genetic predisposition for criminal behavior. Another researcher, Patterson, believes that lack of parental discipline results in antisocial behaviors. Patterson found that antisocial behaviors resulted from a lack of parental monitoring, inconsistent discipline, and failure to teach both social and academic skills. (**Disruptive disorders**)

24. It appears that the most promising treatments are ones that offer training in social and cognitive skills. Children in these types of treatment are taught verbal skills, cooperative play, problem-solving skills and positive social skills. Parent training programs also appear to be successful. Parents learn how to establish rules for the child, provide consequences and provide rewards for positive behaviors. (**Disruptive disorders**)

25. Oppositional defiant disorder is characterized by negative, argumentative and hostile behaviors such as losing one's temper, blaming others, anger, parent-child conflict and refusing to take responsibility for his/her behavior. There is defiance toward authority figures. These behaviors must result in impaired social or academic functioning in order for a diagnosis to be made. (**Disruptive disorders**)

26. The two elimination disorders are encopresis and enuresis. Encopresis is the repeated defecation in inappropriate places by a child who is at least 4 years old. Enuresis is repeated urination into clothes or bedding. Both are typically involuntary. (**Elimination disorders**)

27. Encopresis is the repeated defecation in inappropriate places by a child who is at least 4 years old. Encopresis is more common among males. It is believed to be the result of inadequate toilet training or stress. Encopresis may reoccur intermittently but is rarely chronic. (**Elimination disorders**)

28. The main feature of enuresis is repeated urination during day or night into bed or clothes. Most often this is involuntary. This occurs at least twice per week for three months or must cause distress or impairment in social, academic or occupational functioning. The chronological age of the child is at least 5 years of age. The behavior is not the result of substance use or a medical condition. (**Elimination disorders**)

Grade Yourself

Circle the numbers of the questions you missed, then fill in the total incorrect for each topic. If you answered more than three questions incorrectly, you need to focus on that topic. (If a topic has fewer than three questions and you had at least one wrong, we suggest you study that topic also. Read your textbook or a review book, or ask your teacher for help.)

Subject: Disorders of Childhood and Adolescence

Topic	Question Numbers	Number Incorrect
Attention deficit disorder	1, 8, 9, 10, 11, 15, 16, 17, 18, 19, 20	
Disruptive disorders	2, 3, 4, 12, 13, 14, 21, 22, 23, 24, 25	
Elimination disorders	5, 6, 7, 26, 27, 28	

Mental Retardation, Learning Disorders, and Autism

6

Brief Yourself

Mental retardation involves having significantly below average intellectual functioning (an IQ of 70 or less) with onset prior to age 18 and impaired adaptive functioning. There are four categories of mental retardation: mild, moderate, severe and profound. *Learning disorders* are indicated by below age or intellectual level academic functioning. Specific disorders are reading disorder, mathematics disorder, and disorder of written expression. *Motor skills disorder*, namely developmental coordination disorder, is characterized by below age or intellectual level motor coordination. *Communication disorders* are distinguished by problems with speech or language. These disorders include expressive language disorder, mixed receptive-expressive language disorder, phonological disorder, and stuttering. *Pervasive developmental disorders* consist of severe deficits and impairment in many developmental areas. There may be impaired social interaction and communication and stereotyped behaviors. These disorders include autistic disorder, Rett's disorder, childhood disintegrative disorder, and Asperger's disorder.

Test Yourself

Define the terms in questions 1–11.

1. Learning disorders

2. Adaptive functioning

3. Developmental coordination disorder

4. Communication disorders

5. Expressive language

6. Receptive language

7. Stuttering

8. Pervasive developmental disorders

9. Autism

10. Stereotyped behavior

11. Asperger's disorder

Questions 12–27 are true-false.

12. Mental retardation is defined only by IQ level.

13. Mental retardation can have onset after age 18.

14. Self-care and using community resources are examples of adaptive functioning skills.

15. Moderate mental retardation reflects an IQ between 55 and 70 and is the largest segment of those with mental retardation (85 percent).

16. Those with profound retardation have an IQ below 20 or 25 and represent the smallest group of mentally retarded, about 1 percent.

17. In about 65 percent of cases of mental retardation there is no clear etiology.

18. About 5 percent of cases of mental retardation may be to medical conditions in infancy such as infections or lead poisoning.

19. The prevalence of mental retardation is estimated to be about 1 percent.

20. Children with learning disorders have a high school drop out rate of about 10 percent.

21. About 5 percent of U.S. public school students are estimated to have a learning disorder.

22. Children with expressive language disorder have a limited vocabulary, trouble recalling words and difficulty understanding words or sentences.

23. Children with phonological disorder may substitute one sound for another, omit sounds or lisp.

24. Stress or anxiety may make stuttering worse.

25. Autistic children may lack an awareness of other people.

26. There is no relationship between autism and mental retardation.

27. Rett's disorder has been diagnosed only in females.

28. What are the three diagnostic criteria for mental retardation?

29. What is meant by the term "adaptive functioning?"

30. Distinguish between the four categories of mental retardation.

31. What causes mental retardation?

32. What are learning disorders?

33. What are the three names of the specific learning disorders?

34. What is the developmental coordination disorder?

35. What kinds of problems do children with developmental coordination disorder experience?

36. What is expressive language disorder?

37. What types of language problems do children with expressive language disorder have?

38. What is mixed receptive-expressive language disorder?

39. What is the phonological disorder?

40. Describe stuttering.

41. What are pervasive developmental disorders?

42. Describe autism.

43. What type of social impairment characterizes autism?

44. What type of communication impairment typifies autism?

45. What is meant by "stereotyped behavior"?

46. Is autism related to mental retardation?

47. What are Rett's disorder and Asperger's disorder?

48. What is childhood disintegrative disorder?

Check Yourself

1. Learning disorders are indicated by below age or intellectual level academic functioning affecting reading, math and written expression. (**Learning disorders**)

2. Adaptive functioning is one area of impairment required for a diagnosis of mental retardation which refers to how effectively people deal with life demands and standards of personal autonomy. Adaptive functioning may include communication skills, personal hygiene, home living, social skills, using community resources, self-direction, academic skills, work, leisure, and safety skills. (**Mental retardation**)

3. Developmental coordination disorder is a motor skills disorder typified by impairment in motor coordination development which interferes with either academic achievement or daily activities. (**Motor skills disorder**)

4. Communication disorders involve significant speech or language difficulties. (**Communication disorders**)

5. Expressive language refers to a child's ability to express himself or herself verbally and includes vocabulary development, verb tense rules, recalling words and expressing ideas. (**Communication disorders**)

6. Receptive language refers to a child's ability to understand spoken language and includes comprehension of words, phrases or sentences. (**Communication disorders**)

7. Stuttering is a communication disorder in which the fluency of speech is at an inappropriate developmental level. Sounds may be repeated or lengthened, pauses within a word may occur, words may be substituted to avoid problematic words, and there may be monosyllabic word repetitions. (**Communication disorders**)

8. These are disorders marked by extreme impairment in several developmental areas, including social interaction, communication skills and stereotyped behaviors. These disorders are apparent in the first few years of life and are associated with some level of mental retardation. (**Pervasive developmental disorders**)

9. Autism is a pervasive developmental disorder characterized by impaired development in social interaction and communication and a limited range of interests. (**Pervasive developmental disorders**)

10. Stereotyped body movements include repetitive movements such as clapping, rocking, or swaying. Also, it may involve rigid behaviors such as adhering rigidly to routines, having one narrow interest, and preferring sameness. (**Pervasive developmental disorders**)

11. Asperger's disorder is a pervasive developmental disorder marked by severe and lasting impairment in social interaction and the development of restricted, repetitive behaviors or interests. However, there are no significant delays in language, cognitive, or adaptive skill development. (**Pervasive developmental disorders**)

12. **False.** Mental retardation is defined by three diagnostic criteria: IQ level, adaptive functioning and age at onset. (**Mental retardation**)

13. **False.** Mental retardation can have onset *before* age 18. (**Mental retardation**)

14. **True.** Self-care and using community resources are examples of adaptive functioning skills. **(Mental retardation)**

15. **False.** Mild mental retardation reflects an IQ between 55 and 70 and is the largest segment of those with mental retardation (85 percent). **(Mental retardation)**

16. **True.** Those with profound retardation have an IQ below 20 or 25 and represent the smallest group of mentally retarded, about 1 percent. **(Mental retardation)**

17. **False.** In about *35 percent* of cases of mental retardation there is no clear etiology. **(Mental retardation)**

18. **True.** About 5 percent of cases of mental retardation may be due to medical conditions in infancy such as infections or lead poisoning. **(Mental retardation)**

19. **True.** The prevalence of mental retardation is estimated to be about 1 percent. **(Mental retardation)**

20. **False.** Children with learning disorders have a high school drop out rate of about *40 percent.* **(Learning disorders)**

21. **True.** About 5 percent of U.S. public school students are estimated to have a learning disorder. **(Learning disorders)**

22. **False.** Children with mixed expressive-receptive language disorder have a limited vocabulary, trouble recalling words and difficulty understanding words or sentences. **(Communication disorders)**

23. **True.** Children with phonological disorder may substitute one sound for another, omit sounds or lisp. **(Communication disorders)**

24. **True.** Stress or anxiety may make stuttering worse. **(Communication disorders)**

25. **True.** Autistic children may lack an awareness of other people. **(Pervasive developmental disorders)**

26. **False.** There is a relationship between autism and mental retardation, with about 75 percent of those with autism also diagnosed as mentally retarded. **(Pervasive developmental disorders)**

27. **True.** Rett's disorder has been diagnosed only in females. **(Pervasive developmental disorders)**

28. The three diagnostic criteria for mental retardation are (a) significantly below average intellectual functioning, which means an IQ score of 70 or less, (b) deficiencies in adaptive functioning, and (c) onset prior to age 18. **(Mental retardation)**

29. Adaptive functioning refers to how effectively people deal with common life demands and meet standards of personal independence expected of someone of the same age and background. Adaptive functioning includes such skills as social and daily living skills. **(Mental retardation)**

30. The four categories of mental retardation are mild, moderate, severe and profound retardation. These levels are based on IQ scores. The mildly retarded typically have an IQ between 55 and 70 and represent most of the mentally retarded. These individuals may function at about a sixth-grade level. Even as adults, those who are mildly retarded will require supervision. The moderately retarded usually have an IQ between 40 and 55 and represent about one-tenth of those who are retarded. These individuals function at about the second-grade level and can perform semi-skilled work. The moderately retarded can live in a community setting under supervision. Those people with severe retardation have an IQ between 25 and

40. These people can speak, take care of themselves and perform simple tasks under close guidance. Most of these individuals live in group homes. Those individuals with severe retardation have an IQ below 20 and represent about 1 percent of the mentally retarded. These individuals can learn motor skills and self-care. The American Association on Mental Retardation no longer uses these categories. Instead, they classify people according to how much support they need to function. (**Mental retardation**)

31. Mental retardation may be the result of environmental or genetic factors. There may be genetic variations, chromosomal abnormalities (such as Down's syndrome), malnutrition, infection or premature birth. Fetal alcohol syndrome contributes to children who are born with physical and mental deficiencies. Environmental factors include the absence of stimulation, neglect by parents, chronic stress, poverty, and lack of good health care. (**Mental retardation**)

32. Learning disorders are diagnosed when achievement in reading, mathematics or writing are below expected levels. The level of performance expected is based on the child's age, education and intelligence level. It is believed that about 5 percent of public school children have learning disorders. The deficiency is usually apparent by first or second grade. It is likely that children with learning disorders have relatives with learning disorders. (**Learning disorders**)

33. Specific learning disorders are the reading disorder, mathematics disorder, and disorder of written expression. (**Learning disorders**)

34. Developmental coordination disorder is a motor skills disorder that is characterized by significant impairment in motor coordination that interferes markedly with either academic achievement or daily activities. (**Motor skills disorder**)

35. Young children may be clumsy and experience delays in walking or crawling. Older children may experience problems in motor coordination such as building models, playing ball, or handwriting. (**Motor skills disorder**)

36. Expressive language disorder is a communication disorder typified by an impairment in expressive language development, which may occur in verbal or sign language communication. The communication problem interferes with academic, occupational or social functioning. (**Communication disorders**)

37. Children with expressive language disorder may have a limited vocabulary, make errors in verb tense, and have trouble recalling words and expressing ideas. (**Communication disorders**)

38. Mixed receptive-expressive language disorder is a communication disorder typified by an impairment in both receptive and expressive language development, which may occur in verbal or sign language communication, and interferes with academic, occupational, or social functioning. (**Communication disorders**)

39. Phonological disorder is a communication disorder, formerly called developmental articulation disorder, characterized by a failure to use developmentally appropriate speech sounds. The difficulties in sound production must interfere with academic, occupational or social functioning. (**Communication disorders**)

40. Stuttering is a communication disorder in which the fluency and time patterning of speech is inappropriate for the child's age. This problem interferes with academic, occupational, or social functioning. (**Communication disorders**)

41. Pervasive developmental disorders are marked by extreme impairment in several developmental areas, such as social interaction and communication skills and stereotyped behaviors. These disorders include autism, Rett's disorder, childhood disintegrative disorder, and Asperger's disorder. These disorders are

evident in the first few years of life and are associated with some level of mental retardation. (**Pervasive developmental disorders**)

42. Austism is a pervasive developmental disorder characterized by abnormal or impaired development in social interaction and communication and a limited range of interests. (**Pervasive developmental disorders**)

43. Behaviors used to regulate social interaction, such as eye contact, facial expression, and body language, are significantly impaired. They may not participate in games, preferring solitary activities. These children may lack an awareness of other people. (**Pervasive developmental disorders**)

44. Austistic children may be slower in acquiring speech or not develop speech at all. There is a lack of spontaneous social interaction or pretend play. The pitch, rate or rhythm of speech may be abnormal. There may also be an inability to understand simple instructions. (**Pervasive developmental disorders**)

45. Austistic children may adhere rigidly to routines or rituals. They may engage in repetitive motor activities or be preoccupied with parts of objects. They may have one narrow interest. They may resist change and prefer sameness. Stereotyped body movements include repetitive movements such as clapping, rocking, or swaying. These children may become highly attached to an inanimate object. (**Pervasive developmental disorders**)

46. Yes, about three-fourths of autistic children function at a retarded level. In most cases, there is a diagnosis of moderate mental retardation. (**Pervasive developmental disorders**)

47. Rett's disorder is characterized by multiple deficits that appear after a period of normal functioning after birth. There is normal development in first 5 months of life. However, between ages of 5 and 48 months, head growth slows down and stereotyped hand movements develop. Social interests diminish after onset of this disorder and problems in gait coordination increase. Additionally, severe impairment in expressive and receptive language and motor coordination occurs. This disorder is usually associated with severe or profound mental retardation. Asperger's disorder is a pervasive developmental disorder marked by severe and persistent impairment in social interaction and the development of restricted, repetitive behaviors or interests. There are no delays in language, cognitive, or adaptive skill development. Not much is known about its prevalence, although it appears to be more common among males than among females. (**Pervasive developmental disorders**)

48. The childhood disintegrative disorder is typified by regression in many areas of functioning following at least 2 years of normal functioning. Between the ages of 2 and 10 years, the child experiences significant loss of skills in at least two of these areas: expressive or receptive language, social skills or adaptive behavior, bowel or bladder control, play, or motor skills. There are also social and communication deficits usually seen in autism. This disorder is usually associated with severe mental retardation. (**Pervasive developmental disorders**)

Grade Yourself

Circle the numbers of the questions you missed, then fill in the total incorrect for each topic. If you answered more than three questions incorrectly, you need to focus on that topic. (If a topic has fewer than three questions and you had at least one wrong, we suggest you study that topic also. Read your textbook or a review book, or ask your teacher for help.)

Subject: *Mental Retardation, Learning Disabilities, and Autism*

Topic	Question Numbers	Number Incorrect
Learning disorders	1, 20, 21, 32, 33	
Mental retardation	2, 12, 13, 14, 15, 16, 17, 18, 19, 28, 29, 30, 31	
Motor skills disorder	3, 34, 35	
Communication disorders	4, 5, 6, 7, 22, 23, 24, 36, 37, 38, 39, 40	
Pervasive developmental disorders	8, 9, 10, 11, 25, 26, 27, 41, 42, 43, 44, 45, 46, 47, 48	

Eating Disorders

7

Brief Yourself

Eating disorders are designated by severe disturbances in eating behaviors. There are two types of eating disorders: *anorexia nervosa* and *bulimia nervosa*. Anorexia nervosa is depicted by a refusal to maintain minimum body weight while bulimia nervosa is characterized by repeated periods of binge eating followed by compensatory behaviors such as vomiting, fasting, laxative misuse and/or excessive exercise. Both disorders are also characterized by a disturbed body image. Obesity is not considered an eating disorder in the DSM-IV because there is no compelling evidence that obesity is related to a psychological syndrome.

Test Yourself

Define the terms in questions 1–5.

1. Amenorrheic

2. Anorexia nervosa

3. Bulimia nervosa

4. Binge eating

5. Compensatory behaviors

Questions 6–16 are true-false.

6. Anorexic females may be amenorrheic.

7. Anorexics have a realistic body image.

8. Less than minimal weight refers to weighing less than 25 percent of your expected body weight.

9. Anorexics never purge food.

10. Anorexics' and bulimics' self-esteem depends upon their body shape and weight.

11. More than 90 percent of cases of anorexia nervosa occur in males.

12. Anorexia is most common in the United States and Mexico.

13. The binge eating/purging type of anorexics are more likely to have impulse control problems.

14. Continual snacking on small amounts of food for hours is considered a binge.

15. Binge eating is usually accompanied by a sense of control.

16. The most commonly used compensatory method of bulimics is vomiting.

17. Describe anorexia nervosa.

18. What is meant by "minimal body weight"?

19. How is weight loss accomplished by anorexic individuals?

20. How is their self-image distorted?

21. What are the subtypes of anorexia nervosa?

22. Describe bulimia nervosa.

23. What is meant by "binge eating"?

24. What kinds of "compensatory behaviors" are used by bulimics?

25. How is their self-image distorted?

26. What are the subtypes of bulimia nervosa?

 # Check Yourself

1. After menarche, menstrual periods cease due to a lack of nutrition. (**Anorexia nervosa**)

2. Anorexia nervosa is an eating disorder typified by a refusal to maintain minimal body weight, a fear of weight gain, and a distorted perception of the physical body. (**Anorexia nervosa**)

3. Bulimia nervosa is an eating disorder typified by binge eating and compensatory behaviors designed to inhibit weight gain. (**Bulimia nervosa**)

4. A binge occurs when, in a limited time period, a person eats much more food than most people would under similar circumstances. (**Bulimia nervosa**)

5. Compensatory behaviors, such as vomiting, misuse of laxatives, fasting, or exercising, are supposed to inhibit weight gain. (**Bulimia nervosa**)

6. **True.** Anorexic females may be amenorrheic. (**Anorexia nervosa**)

7. **False.** Anorexics have a *distorted* body image. (**Anorexia nervosa**)

8. **False.** Less than minimal weight refers to weighing less than *85 percent* of your expected body weight. (**Anorexia nervosa**)

9. **False.** Anorexics *sometimes* purge food. (**Anorexia nervosa**)

10. **True.** The anorexics' and bulimics' self-esteem depends upon their body shape and weight. (**Anorexia nervosa**)

11. **False.** More than 90 percent of cases of anorexia nervosa occur in *females*. (**Anorexia nervosa**)

12. **False.** Anorexia is most common in the United States, Canada, Europe, Australia, Japan, New Zealand and South Africa. (**Anorexia nervosa**)

13. **True.** The *binge eating/purging* type of anorexics are more likely to have impulse control problems. (**Bulimia nervosa**)

14. **False.** Continual snacking on small amounts of food for hours is *not* considered a binge. (**Bulimia nervosa**)

15. **False.** Binge eating is usually accompanied by a sense of *lack of* control. (**Bulimia nervosa**)

16. **True.** The most commonly used compensatory method of bulimics is vomiting. (**Bulimia nervosa**)

17. Anorexia nervosa is an eating disorder in which there is a refusal to maintain minimal body weight, a fear of weight gain, and a distorted perception of the body. Additionally, females who have begun menstruating are amenorrheic (stop having menstrual periods). This disorder may involve either weight loss or failure to gain weight. (**Anorexia nervosa**)

18. A person weighing less than 85 percent of the expected body weight (based on age and height) meets the criteria for being underweight, or having a less than minimal body weight. (**Anorexia nervosa**)

19. Typically, anorexics eat less food in order to lose weight. Additionally, they may purge themselves of food by vomiting or use of laxatives, or they may exercise to an excessive degree. (**Anorexia nervosa**)

20. Anorexics may feel overweight or feel that certain parts of their body are too fat. Anorexics' self-esteem depends upon their body shape and weight. Weight loss is perceived as a sign of self-discipline while weight gain is perceived as a sign of lack of self-control. (**Anorexia nervosa**)

21. The two subtypes of anorexia nervosa are the *restricting type* and the *binge eating/purging type*. The restricting type anorexics lose weight by dieting, fasting or exercise without regularly binge eating or purging. The binge eating/purging type describes a person who regularly binges or purges (or both). (**Anorexia nervosa**)

22. Bulimia nervosa is an eating disorder in which there is persistent binge eating and compensatory behaviors designed to limit weight gain. The self-evaluation of bulimics is very much influenced by body shape and weight. (**Bulimia nervosa**)

23. A binge occurs when, in a small time period, a person eats much more food than most people would under similar circumstances. Continual snacking on small amounts of food for hours is not considered a binge. A binge usually occurs within a two-hour period and involves eating a lot of food. The kind of food eaten is usually sweet and very high in calories. Binge eating usually occurs in secrecy and is usually accompanied by a sense of lack of control. (**Bulimia nervosa**)

24. The most commonly used compensatory method is vomiting after a binge episode, used by 80 percent to 90 percent of bulimics. About one-third of bulimics will misuse laxatives after binge eating. Some bulimics will fast or exercise excessively. (**Bulimia nervosa**)

25. Bulimics place too much emphasis on body shape and weight in determining their self-esteem. They, like anorexics, fear gaining weight and are dissatisfied with their bodies. (**Bulimia nervosa**)

26. The two subtypes of anorexia nervosa are the purging type and the nonpurging type. The purging type bulimics regularly use vomiting, laxatives or enemas to lose weight. The nonpurging type use other compensatory methods, such as fasting or exercise, but has not regularly used vomiting, laxatives or enemas to lose weight. (**Bulimia nervosa**)

Grade Yourself

Circle the numbers of the questions you missed, then fill in the total incorrect for each topic. If you answered more than three questions incorrectly, you need to focus on that topic. (If a topic has fewer than three questions and you had at least one wrong, we suggest you study that topic also. Read your textbook or a review book, or ask your teacher for help.)

Subject: Eating Disorders

Topic	Question Numbers	Number Incorrect
Anorexia nervosa	1, 2, 6, 7, 8, 9, 10, 11, 12, 17, 18, 19, 20, 21	
Bulimia nervosa	3, 4, 5, 13, 14, 15, 16, 22, 23, 24, 25, 26	

Anxiety Disorders

8

Brief Yourself

Anxiety is an emotional state typified by negative affect and tension symptoms. A person who is anxious usually envisions future danger. Moderate amounts of anxiety are helpful in preparing us for performance activities. *Anxiety disorders* are all characterized by the main symptom of anxiety; however, they differ in terms of what the anxiety is focused on, or how that anxiety is expressed. The anxiety disorders include *panic disorders* (with or without agoraphobia), *agoraphobia, specific phobia, social phobia, obsessive-compulsive disorder, post-traumatic stress disorder, acute stress disorder, generalized anxiety disorder, anxiety disorder* (due to a medical condition), and *substance-induced anxiety disorder. Panic disorders* are typified by recurrent panic attacks, with or without *agoraphobia.* Agoraphobia refers to being anxious about or avoiding places in which escape is hard or in which help is unavailable (for panic attacks). Specific phobias are characterized by marked anxiety in presence of a feared object. Social phobia refers to significant anxiety brought on by exposure to social or performance situations. Obsessive-compulsive disorder is typified by recurrent thoughts or behaviors that either cause anxiety or alleviate anxiety. Post-traumatic stress disorder involves reliving a traumatic event, accompanied by anxiety symptoms and avoidance behaviors. Acute stress disorder is marked by anxiety symptoms that occur immediately subsequent to a very traumatic event. Generalized anxiety disorder is characterized by at least six months of excessive anxiety.

Test Yourself

Define the terms in questions 1–10.

1. Panic attack

2. Derealization

3. Depersonalization

4. Paresthesias

5. Agoraphobia

6. Acrophobia

7. Obsessions

8. Compulsions

9. Generalized social phobia

10. Omen formation

Questions 11–18 are true-false.

11. In some cultures, panic attacks may be related to an intense fear of witchcraft or magic.

12. About three-fourths of those with panic disorder have agoraphobia.

13. The diagnosis of panic disorder requires at least two panic attacks.

14. The situational type of specific phobia refers to fears of animals or insects.

15. The natural environment type of specific phobia refers to fear brought on by storms, heights, or water and also has an adult onset.

16. Typically the onset of social phobia is midadolescence, developing out of a history of shyness or inhibition.

17. A person with obsessive-compulsive disorder recognizes that the obsessions or compulsions are excessive or irrational.

18. Panic disorders are more common in men than women.

19. What is a panic attack?

20. What are the three types of panic attacks?

21. Describe agoraphobia.

22. What is panic disorder?

23. What causes panic disorders?

24. How are panic disorders treated?

25. What are some of the causes of phobias?

26. Describe specific phobia.

27. What are the subtypes of specific phobia?

28. What is social phobia?

29. How are social phobia treated?

30. Describe obsessive-compulsive disorder.

31. What kinds of compulsive behaviors or rituals are most common in OCD?

32. What may cause OCD?

33. How is OCD treated?

34. Describe post-traumatic stress disorder.

35. What causes PTSD?

36. How is PTSD treated?

37. Describe generalized anxiety disorder.

38. What are possible treatments for GAD?

Check Yourself

1. Panic attacks are a marked specific period of intense fear that is accompanied by at least four out of thirteen cognitive or somatic symptoms. **(Panic disorders)**

2. Derealization is a component of panic attacks and involves a person experiencing feelings of unreality. **(Panic disorders)**

3. Depersonalization is another component of panic attacks and involves a person experiencing feelings of being detached from himself or herself. **(Panic disorders)**

4. Paresthesias often occur in panic attacks and involve a numbness or tingling sensation felt by the individual. **(Panic disorders)**

5. Agoraphobia refers to anxiety about being in places where escape is difficult or embarrassing or in which is not available in event of a panic attack. **(Panic disorders)**

6. Acrophobia refers to a fear of heights. **(Phobias)**

7. Obsessions are reoccurring intrusive and irrational thoughts or urges that one may resist or attempt to expel. **(Obsessive-compulsive disorder)**

8. Compulsions are repeated ritualistic and time-consuming actions that a person feels driven to carry out. Compulsions can also be mental actions such as counting. **(Obsessive-compulsive disorder)**

9. Generalized social phobia refers to fearing most social situations. **(Phobias)**

10. Sometimes children with post-traumatic stress disorder experience omen formation, a belief that they can foresee future disturbing events. **(Post-traumatic stress disorder)**

11. **True.** In some cultures, panic attacks may be related to an intense fear of witchcraft or magic. **(Panic disorders)**

12. **False.** About *one-third to one-half* of those with panic disorder have agoraphobia. **(Panic disorders)**

13. **True.** The diagnosis of panic disorder requires at least two panic attacks. **(Panic disorders)**

14. **False.** The situational type of specific phobia refers to fears caused by situations like public transportation, tunnels, bridges, elevators, driving or enclosed spaces. **(Phobias)**

15. **False.** The natural environment type of specific phobia refers to fear brought on by storms, heights, or water and also has *childhood* onset. **(Phobias)**

16. **True.** Typically the onset of social phobia is midadolescence, developing out of a history of shyness or inhibition. **(Phobias)**

17. **True.** A person with obsessive-compulsive disorder recognizes that the obsessions or compulsions are excessive or irrational. **(Obsessive-compulsive disorder)**

18. **False.** Panic disorders are more common in *women than men*. **(Panic disorders)**

19. Panic attacks involve intense fear coupled with symptoms such as heart pounding, trembling, breathing difficulties, and fear of losing control or dying. Panic attacks are sudden and often accompanied by a desire to flee. Panic attacks occur in several anxiety disorders. **(Panic disorders)**

20. There are three different kinds of panic attacks: unexpected panic attacks, situationally bound panic attacks, and situationally predisposed panic attacks. The unexpected panic attacks occur without any apparent cause, spontaneously. The situationally bound panic attacks occur immediately upon being exposed to a feared stimulus, always in presence of the same stimulus. The situationally predisposed panic attacks may occur in presence of a stimulus but not always. **(Panic disorders)**

21. Agoraphobia is an intense fear of being in public places where help may not be available. Paniclike symptoms incapacitate the person and cause him or her to faint or display fear in public. The anxiety over having these symptoms is so intense it may hinder people from leaving their homes. **(Panic disorders)**

22. Panic disorders are characterized by repeated panic attacks (at least two) and then worry about having another panic attack. The panic attacks are usually unexpected. **(Panic disorders)**

23. Many people with panic disorders report having a childhood that involved intense separation anxiety, family conflicts and academic problems. Others state that their panic attacks occurred after leaving home or losing a loved one. Exposure to major life changes may also bring about panic attacks. Women are two to three times more likely to be diagnosed with a panic disorder than men. **(Panic disorders)**

24. Panic disorders can be treated with medication that affects the neurotransmitters serotonin, norepinephrine, or GABA. Drugs that affect these systems are benzodiazepines and tricyclic antidepressants, which seem to be equally effective. As long as medication is taken, about 60 percent of those with panic disorder remain free of panic symptoms. There is a high relapse rate when medication is stopped: about 90 percent relapse when benzodiazepines are ceased and almost half relapse when tricyclics are stopped. **(Panic disorders)**

25. Phobias may be due to four possible causes. One is that phobias are acquired through direct experience with the feared object. Another possibility is that a person experiences a false alarm (panic attack) in a specific situation. People may also acquire phobias vicariously, by observing someone else experience fear. Last, people may develop phobias when they are provided with information about a dangerous object. **(Phobias)**

26. Specific phobia refers to an extreme fear of a specific object or situations that interferes with a person's ability to function or causes distress. Exposure to this specific object nearly always causes anxiety. Adults or adolescents may recognize that the fear is irrational or excessive. **(Phobias)**

27. The subtypes of specific phobia, which are used to indicate the feared object, are: *animal type, natural environment type, blood injection-injury type, situational type*, or *other type*. The animal type involves fear caused by animals or insects and usually begins in childhood. The natural environment type, which also begins in childhood, refers to fear brought on by storms, heights, or water. The blood injection-injury type refers to a fear caused by seeing blood or injury or receiving an injection. The situational type refers to fears caused by situations such as public transportation, tunnels, bridges, elevators, driving or enclosed spaces. The other type is a category which includes fears of choking or vomiting and fear of falling down if away from walls. **(Phobias)**

28. Social phobia is a persistent fear of social or performance situations which may result in humiliation and anxiety. Adults and adolescents realize that this fear may be irrational or excessive; however, most

children do not realize this. Most often the situation is avoided. Usually social phobia originate in midadolescence, developing out of a history of shyness or inhibition. (**Phobias**)

29. Social phobia can be treated psychologically using a therapy in which clients role-play anxiety-provoking situations in front of a group. Additionally, cognitive behavior therapy is used to uncover and modify perceptions that danger exists in these feared situations. There are also drug treatments for social phobia. Tricyclic antidepressants and MAO inhibitors are both more effective than placebos; however, there is a high relapse rate when the drugs are discontinued. (**Phobias**)

30. Obsessive-compulsive disorder (OCD) is characterized by chronic obsessions or compulsions that are time consuming or cause significant distress or impairment. The person will attempt to ignore, suppress or eliminate such thoughts or actions. Additionally, the person recognizes that the obsessions or compulsions are excessive or irrational, being created by the person's mind. Most people with OCD are female. OCD tends to be chronic. (**Obsessive-compulsive disorder**)

31. Research has determined that the most common OCD obsessions are contamination obsessions, aggressive urges, sexual urges, bodily complaints, and the need for order or perfection. Many people with OCD experience many obsessions. (**Obsessive-compulsive disorder**)

32. One idea is that people with OCD learn as children that certain thoughts are dangerous and they equate these thoughts with the specific behaviors symbolized by the thoughts. Then the person attempts not to think about these thoughts. The more they try to suppress thoughts, the harder it becomes to do so. Additionally, there are probably physiological and psychological vulnerabilities that predispose some people to develop OCD. (**Obsessive-compulsive disorder**)

33. Medication studies reveal hope that drugs can help alleviate OCD. The most effective drugs seem to target the reuptake of serotonin, a neurotransmitter, such as fluoxetine (Prozac). However, there is a high probability of relapse if medication is stopped. Some psychological treatments, referred to as exposure and response prevention, also appear to have moderate success. This approach tries to prevent the rituals and gradually expose the person to the feared thoughts. The rituals are prevented through close observation and supervision. People with OCD learn that no harm results from not engaging in these behaviors. Another more extreme method of treatment is psychosurgery. Often a surgical lesion to a part of the brain (the cingulate bundle) is used as a last resort for those for whom all other treatments have failed. (**Obsessive-compulsive disorder**)

34. Post-traumatic stress disorder (PTSD) results from a specific stressful, traumatic event, lasts longer than one month, and involves intrusive memories of the traumatic event, emotional withdrawal, and increased physiological arousal. The traumatic event may be life-threatening such as combat experiences, abductions, rape, incest, natural disasters, and concentration camp experiences. Most people become numb emotionally and avoid anything that will trigger memories of the traumatic event. Also, people with PTSD may have insomnia, anxiety attacks, hyperalertness and aggressive behavior. (**Post-traumatic stress disorder**)

35. In the etiology of PTSD, the intensity of the traumatic experience is important. The greater a person's biological and psychological vulnerability, the more likely he or she will develop PTSD. If anxiety runs in a family, then family members may be biologically predisposed to develop PTSD. At lower levels of trauma, a person's psychological vulnerability plays a larger role in developing PTSD. At higher levels of trauma, most people will develop PTSD. Also, having a strong support network makes a person less likely to develop PTSD. (**Post-traumatic stress disorder**)

36. Psychotherapy involves re-exposing the person to the initial trauma in order to deal with and overcome the effects of the trauma. Additionally, drug treatments are now being tested to determine their efficacy in dealing with PTSD. (**Post-traumatic stress disorder**)

37. Generalized anxiety disorder (GAD) is identified by persistent high levels of anxiety and excessive worry for at least six months. There are physiological symptoms such as heart palpitations, trembling, restlessness, sleep difficulties, apprehension, nervousness and poor concentration. People with GAD worry about minor and major life concerns. Those people who are older, separated, widowed, divorced or unemployed are at greater risk for GAD than others. (**Generalized anxiety disorder**)

38. GAD may have a biological component, as it tends to run in families. Also, those with GAD are different from clients with other anxiety disorders, such as panic disorder, in that people with GAD do not have strong sympathetic nervous system arousal. Those with GAD exhibit less physiological responsiveness in general than those with other anxiety disorders. When GAD clients are compared to nonanxious people, the main difference is that those with GAD are chronically tense. Because of these factors, it is believed that people with GAD are more aware of potential threats at an unconscious level. Other evidence shows that GAD clients have intense frontal lobe left-hemisphere brain wave activity, which suggests intense cognitive activity without mental images. They are busy thinking about the threat but do so without images, which would create more negative emotions. So perhaps this restricted affect leads to a state of muscle tension without the accompanying sympathetic arousal one would expect when faced with a threat. The person with GAD is avoiding dealing with the perceived threat much like a person with a phobia tries to avoid the feared object. (**Generalized anxiety disorder**)

Grade Yourself

Circle the numbers of the questions you missed, then fill in the total incorrect for each topic. If you answered more than three questions incorrectly, you need to focus on that topic. (If a topic has fewer than three questions and you had at least one wrong, we suggest you study that topic also. Read your textbook or a review book, or ask your teacher for help.)

Subject: Anxiety Disorders

Topic	Question Numbers	Number Incorrect
Panic disorders	1, 2, 3, 4, 5, 11, 12, 13, 18, 19, 20, 21, 22, 23, 24	
Phobias	6, 9, 14, 15, 16, 25, 26, 27, 28, 29	
Obsessive-compulsive disorder	7, 8, 17, 30, 31, 32, 33	
Post-traumatic stress disorder	10, 34, 35, 36	
Generalized anxiety disorder	37, 38	

Somatoform and Factitious Disorders

9

Brief Yourself

Somatoform disorders are characterized by physical symptoms that suggest a medical condition but are not caused by a medical condition, the effects of a substance, or another mental disorder. These symptoms must cause significant distress and functional impairment. The physical symptoms of somatoform disorders are involuntary, in contrast to the voluntary symptoms of factitious disorders. Somatoform disorders include somatization disorder, conversion disorder, pain disorder, hypochondriasis and body dysmorphic disorder. Somatization disorder is a multiple-symptom disorder, with onset prior to age 30, lasting many years, exemplified by a combination of pain, gastrointestinal, sexual and pseudoneurological symptoms. Conversion disorder is characterized by unexplained symptoms affecting voluntary motor or sensory function that suggest a neurological or medical condition. Psychological factors are believed to cause these symptoms. Pain disorder involves pain, as well as psychological factors that affect the severity of this disorder. Hypochondriasis is the fixation with the fear of having a serious disease based on misinterpretation of symptoms. Body dysmorphic disorder is the preoccupation with an imagined or distorted defect in physical appearance. *Factitious disorders* are characterized by physical or psychological symptoms that are intentionally produced in order to assume the patient role. The judgment that a particular symptom is intentionally produced is made both by direct evidence and exclusion of other causes. It should be noted that the presence of factitious symptoms does not necessarily preclude the coexistence of true physical or psychological symptoms.

Test Yourself

Define the terms in questions 1–5.

1. Clinically significant complaint

2. Conversion symptoms

3. Dissociative symptoms

4. Hypochondriasis

5. Factitious disorders

Questions 6–17 are true-false.

6. The somatic complaints of a somatization disorder must begin after age 30 and occur over a period of two years.

7. In a somatization disorder, there must be a history of several sexual or reproductive symptoms.

8. Conversion disorder is reported to be more common in urban areas and among people of higher socioeconomic status.

9. Nausea or abdominal bloating are not two of the possible gastrointestinal symptoms of somatization disorder.

10. In men, there may be symptoms of erectile or ejaculatory dysfunction in somatization disorder.

11. The symptoms of somatization disorder are intentionally produced.

12. Fainting is a dissociative symptom.

13. Somatization disorder occurs more frequently in Greek and Puerto Rican men, as compared to American men.

14. In women, symptoms of conversion disorder are much more common on the left side of the body.

15. Pain disorder associated with a general medical condition is not considered a mental disorder and is coded on Axis III.

16. Males appear to experience certain chronic pain conditions, most notably headaches and musculoskeletal pain, more often than do females.

17. For those with hypochondriasis, concern about the feared illness often becomes a central feature of the individual's self-image.

18. Describe somatization disorder.

19. Where in the body must pain or symptoms occur in somatization disorder?

20. What kinds of sexual or reproductive symptoms must be present in somatization disorder?

21. What are conversion symptoms?

22. What are dissociative symptoms?

23. What is conversion disorder?

24. What are the subtypes of conversion disorder?

25. What are the main features of pain disorder?

26. What are some examples of how pain can result in impairment?

27. What is the difference between chronic and acute pain disorder?

28. Describe hypochondriasis.

29. What is body dysmorphic disorder?

30. What are factitious disorders?

Check Yourself

1. A complaint is clinically significant if it results in medical treatment or causes significant impairment in social, occupational, or other areas of functioning. (**Somatization disorders**)

2. Conversion symptoms include impaired coordination or balance, paralysis, difficulty swallowing, urinary retention, hallucinations, loss of touch or pain sensation, double vision, blindness, deafness or seizures. (**Somatization disorders**)

3. Dissociative symptoms may include amnesia or loss of consciousness other than fainting. (**Somatization disorders**)

4. Hypochondriasis is the preoccupation with fears of having, or the idea that one has, a serious disease based on a misinterpretation of bodily symptoms. (**Hypochondriasis**)

5. Factitious disorders are characterized by physical or psychological symptoms that are intentionally produced or feigned in order to assume the sick role. (**Factitious disorders**)

6. **False.** The somatic complaints of a somatization disorder must begin *before* age 30 and occur over a period of several years. (**Somatization disorders**)

7. **False.** In a somatization disorder, must be a history of *at least one* sexual or reproductive symptom. (**Somatization disorders**)

8. **False.** Conversion disorder is reported to be more common in *rural* areas and among people of *lower* socioeconomic status. (**Conversion disorder**)

9. **True.** Nausea or abdominal bloating are not two of the possible gastrointestinal symptoms of somatization disorder. (**Somatization disorders**)

10. **True.** In men, there may be symptoms of erectile or ejaculatory dysfunction in somatization disorder. (**Somatization disorders**)

11. **False.** The symptoms of somatization disorder are *not intentionally* produced. (**Somatization disorders**)

12. **False.** Fainting is *not* a dissociative symptom. Dissociative symptoms may include amnesia or loss of consciousness other than fainting. (**Somatization disorders**)

13. **True.** Somatization disorder occurs more frequently in Greek and Puerto Rican men, as compared to American men. (**Somatization disorders**)

14. **True.** In women, symptoms of conversion disorder are much more common on the left side of the body. (**Conversion disorder**)

15. **True.** Pain disorder associated with a general medical condition is not considered a mental disorder and is coded on Axis III. (**Pain disorder**)

16. **False.** *Females* appear to experience certain chronic pain conditions, most notably headaches and musculoskeletal pain, more often than do *males*. (**Pain disorder**)

17. **True.** For those with hypochondriasis, concern about the feared illness often becomes a central feature of the individual's self-image. (**Hypochondriasis**)

18. Somatization disorder is identified by recurrent, multiple bodily complaints. The bodily complaints must begin before age 30 and occur over a period of several years. These unexplained symptoms are not intentionally produced. (**Somatization disorders**)

19. In somatization disorder, there must be a history of pain related to at least four different sites (head, abdomen, back, joints, extremities, chest, rectum) or functions (menstruation, sexual intercourse, urination). There must also be a history of at least two gastrointestinal symptoms other than pain, such as nausea or abdominal bloating, and at least one sexual or reproductive symptom other than pain. Last, there must be a history of at least one symptom that suggests a neurological condition (such as conversion symptoms or dissociative symptoms). (**Somatization disorders**)

20. In women, this may be irregular menses, menorrhagia, or vomiting throughout pregnancy. In men, there may be symptoms of erectile or ejaculatory dysfunction. (**Somatization disorders**)

21. Conversion symptoms include impaired coordination or balance, paralysis, difficulty swallowing, urinary retention, hallucinations, loss of touch or pain sensation, double vision, blindness, deafness or seizures. (**Somatization disorders**)

22. Dissociative symptoms may include amnesia or loss of consciousness other than fainting. (**Somatization disorders**)

23. The main characteristic of conversion disorder is the presence of symptoms affecting voluntary motor or sensory function that suggest a neurological condition. Symptoms are not intentionally produced or feigned. The problem must cause either marked distress or impaired functioning. (**Conversion disorder**)

24. Motor symptoms or deficits include impaired coordination or balance, paralysis, difficulty swallowing, or urinary retention. Sensory symptoms include loss of touch or pain sensation, double vision, blindness, deafness or hallucinations. (**Conversion disorder**)

25. Pain disorder is typified by pain that causes significant distress or impairment in social, occupational, or other important areas of functioning. Psychological factors play a significant role in the onset, severity, exacerbation, or maintenance of the pain. The pain is unintentionally produced. (**Pain disorder**)

26. Examples of impairment resulting from pain include inability to work or attend school, frequent use of the health care system, the pain becoming a major focus of the individual's life, substantial use of medications, and relationship problems such as marital and family discord. (**Pain disorder**)

27. Acute pain disorder refers to the fact that the duration of the pain is less than 6 months, while chronic pain disorder means that the symptoms last 6 months or more. (**Pain disorder**)

28. Hypochondriasis is a persistent worrying about one's health despite medical evaluations that reveal no physical problems. This disorder includes a fear of having a disease, fear of death, and oversensitivity to bodily sensations. Bodily symptoms are seen as signs of disease despite medical reassurance. Hypochondriasis is usually chronic. (**Hypochondriasis**)

29. The main characteristic of body dysmorphic disorder (historically known as dysmorphobia) is a preoccupation with a defect in appearance. The defect is either imagined or the individual's concern is markedly excessive. (**Body dysmorphic disorder**)

30. Factitious disorders are characterized by physical or psychological symptoms that are intentionally feigned in order to assume the sick role. The judgment that a particular symptom is intentionally produced is made both by direct evidence and by excluding other causes of the symptom. **(Factitious disorder)**

Grade Yourself

Circle the numbers of the questions you missed, then fill in the total incorrect for each topic. If you answered more than three questions incorrectly, you need to focus on that topic. (If a topic has fewer than three questions and you had at least one wrong, we suggest you study that topic also. Read your textbook or a review book, or ask your teacher for help.)

Subject: Somatoform and Factitious Disorders

Topic	Question Numbers	Number Incorrect
Somatization disorders	1, 2, 3, 6, 7, 9, 10, 11, 12, 13, 18, 19, 20, 21, 22	
Hypochondriasis	4, 17, 28	
Factitious disorders	5, 30	
Conversion disorder	8, 14, 23, 24	
Pain disorder	15, 16, 25, 26, 27	
Body dysmorphic disorder	29	

Dissociative Disorders

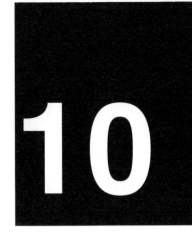

10

Brief Yourself

Dissociative disorders are characterized by a disturbance in the usually integrated functions of consciousness, memory, identity, or perception of the environment. The disturbance may be sudden or gradual, transient or chronic. *Dissociative amnesia* is characterized by an inability to recall important information, usually of a traumatic or stressful nature, that is too extensive to be explained by ordinary forgetfulness. *Dissociative fugue* is characterized by sudden, unexpected travel away from home or one's customary place of work, accompanied by an inability to recall one's past and confusion about personal identity or the assumption of a new identity. *Dissociative identity disorder* (formerly multiple personality disorder) is characterized by the presence of two or more distinct identities or personality states that recurrently take control of the individual's behavior, accompanied by an inability to recall important personal information that is much more extensive than can be explained by ordinary forgetfulness. *Depersonalization disorder* is characterized by a persistent or recurrent feeling of being detached from one's mental processes or body that is accompanied by intact reality testing.

Test Yourself

Define the terms in questions 1–4.

1. Amnesia

2. Fugue

3. Depersonalization disorder

4. Multiple personality disorder

Questions 5–9 are true-false.

5. Dissociative amnesia involves an irreversible memory disturbance in which memories of personal experience cannot be retrieved verbally or remain in consciousness.

6. Dissociative amnesia is not difficult to assess in preadolescent children.

7. In dissociative fugue, there is also confusion about personal identity or even the taking of a new identity.

8. The prevalence of dissociative fugue may decrease during times of war or natural disaster.

9. Individuals with depersonalization disorder may feel like a robot or as if living in a dream.

10. Describe dissociative amnesia.

11. What are the main characteristics of dissociative fugue?

12. What is dissociative identity disorder?

13. Describe depersonalization disorder.

14. What causes dissociative disorders?

Check Yourself

1. Dissociative amnesia is exemplified by an inability to remember important personal information that is too extensive to be explained by forgetfulness. (**Dissociative amnesia**)

2. Dissociative fugue involves sudden, unexpected travel away from one's home or job, with the inability to remember parts of one's past. (**Dissociative fugue**)

3. Depersonalization disorder is typified by persistent or reoccurring episodes of depersonalization characterized by feelings of detachment or estrangement from one's self. (**Depersonalization disorder**)

4. Now known as dissociative identity disorder, it refers to the presence of many identities or personality states that repeatedly take control of an individual's behavior. (**Dissociative identity disorder**)

5. **False.** Dissociative amnesia involves *a reversible* memory disturbance in which memories of personal experience cannot be retrieved verbally or remain in consciousness. (**Dissociative amnesia**)

6. **False.** Dissociative amnesia is *especially difficult* to assess in preadolescent children, because it may be confused with inattention, anxiety, oppositional behavior, learning disorders, psychotic disturbances, and developmentally appropriate childhood amnesia. (**Dissociative amnesia**)

7. **True.** In dissociative fugue, there is also confusion about personal identity or even the taking of a new identity. (**Dissociative fugue**)

8. **False.** The prevalence may *increase* during times of extremely stressful events such as war or natural disaster. (**Dissociative fugue**)

9. **True.** Individuals with depersonalization disorder may feel like a robot or as if living in a dream. (**Depersonalization disorder**)

10. Dissociative amnesia reflects a partial or total loss of important personal information and sometimes happens after a stressful event. The person cannot recall his or her name, address, friends and relatives. There are four types of dissociative amnesia: localized, selective, generalized and continuous. Localized amnesia is the most common and refers to an inability to recall all events within a specific short time period, usually focused on a traumatic event. Selective amnesia is the inability to remember specific details of an event. Generalized amnesia is the failure to remember anything about one's past life. Continuous amnesia is the least common and refers to a failure to remember events that occurred between a specific time in the past and the present. (**Dissociative amnesia**)

11. Dissociative fugue is confusion over personal identity accompanied by unexpected travel away from home. Most cases involve only short periods away from home. Sometimes the person may adopt a new identity. Usually recovery from fugue is abrupt and complete. (**Dissociative fugue**)

12. Dissociative identity disorder was formerly known as multiple personality disorder. This disorder refers to a situation in which at least two distinct, independent personalities appear to exist in one person. Only one personality is evident at any one time and there is amnesia for the personality that is replaced by another. One or more personalities may be aware of the existence of the other personalities. This disorder is much more likely to occur in women, who may report having been physically or sexually abused as a child. (**Dissociative identity disorder**)

13. Depersonalization disorder is identified by a feeling of unreality concerning the self and environment. The diagnosis is made when this unreality causes significant distress or impairment in social or occupational functioning. The person may feels as if the body is distorted or as if he or she is living in a dream. **(Depersonalization disorder)**

14. Dissociative disorders are not well understood. The psychoanalytic perspective states that dissociative disorders may be the result of the use of repression to block traumatic events. When complete repression is not possible, dissociation may occur. In amnesia and fugue, large parts of the person's identity are not conscious thereby protecting the person from painful memories. Dissociative identity disorder (DID) may result from early traumatic experiences combined with one's inability to accept these experiences. One or more personalities take on the painful memories in order to protect the other personalities. Most people with DID report a history of physical or sexual abuse. Behaviorists believe that people with dissociative disorders are unable to handle emotional conflicts so they try to forget or block out painful thoughts. **(Dissociative identity disorder)**

Grade Yourself

Circle the numbers of the questions you missed, then fill in the total incorrect for each topic. If you answered more than three questions incorrectly, you need to focus on that topic. (If a topic has fewer than three questions and you had at least one wrong, we suggest you study that topic also. Read your textbook or a review book, or ask your teacher for help.)

Subject: Dissociative Disorders

Topic	Question Numbers	Number Incorrect
Dissociative amnesia	1, 5, 6, 10	
Dissociative fugue	2, 7, 8, 11	
Depersonalization disorder	3, 9, 13	
Dissociative identity disorder	4, 12, 14	

Mood Disorders

11

Brief Yourself

Mood disorders were once called "depressive" or "affective" disorders. Now these disorders are referred to as mood disorders to reflect the common characteristic of a marked aberration in mood. There are two experiences which contribute to all mood disorders, depression and mania. These experiences are described as episodes, each with its own diagnostic criteria. The most common and most severe episode is major depressive episode. These episodes are characterized by feelings of worthlessness, disruptions in activities and the inability to experience pleasure, which must last at least two weeks. A manic episode is a period of abnormally elevated elation or euphoria. People may experience extreme pleasure and joy from activities and be hyperactive. They may also talk rapidly due to having many ideas at once. There is one more episode, called hypomania, which is less severe a disruption than mania. The diagnosis for major depressive disorder requires at least one major depressive episode, which consists of at least two weeks of depressed mood or loss of interest, accompanied by at least four additional symptoms of depression. Dysthymic disorder is characterized by at least two years of depressed mood for more days than not, accompanied by additional depressive symptoms that do not meet criteria for a major depressive episode. Bipolar disorders used to be called manic-depression. Bipolar I disorder is characterized by one or more manic or mixed episodes, usually accompanied by major depressive episodes.

Test Yourself

Define the terms in questions 1–8.

1. Major depressive episode

2. Manic episode

3. Mixed episode

4. Electroconvulsive therapy

5. Major depressive disorder

6. Dysthymic disorder

7. Cyclothymic disorder

Questions 8–13 are true-false.

8. When diagnosing a major depressive episode, clinicians should ignore symptoms that are cultural norms.

9. In elderly adults, cognitive symptoms may be the most prominent in a major depressive episode.

10. Mixed episodes are more in common in younger individuals and in males than in females.

11. Prevalence rates for major depressive disorder are related to ethnicity, education, income, and marital status.

12. In Major Depression, preadolescent boys and girls are equally affected.

13. In bipolar I, the first episode is more likely to be a manic episode in males and a depressive episode in females.

14. What is a major depressive episode?

15. Are there sex differences with respect to major depressive episodes?

16. What is a manic episode?

17. Describe a mixed episode.

18. How is a hypomanic episode manifested in adolescence?

19. What is major disorder?

20. Are men and women differentially affected by major depression?

21. Describe dysthymic disorder.

22. What are the diagnostic features of bipolar I disorder?

23. What is bipolar II disorder?

24. Describe cyclothymic disorder.

25. What causes mood disorders?

26. How are mood disorders treated?

27. Are there medications for bipolar disorders?

28. What is electroconvulsive therapy?

29. What are the most effective psychological treatments for depressive disorders?

30. What are some factors that increase a person's risk for suicide?

31. Do suicides always occur in clusters?

Check Yourself

1. The most common and most severe episode is major depressive episode. These episodes are characterized by feelings of worthlessness, disruptions in activities and the inability to experience pleasure, which must last at least two weeks. (**Mood disorder episodes**)

2. A manic episode is a period of elevated mood or euphoria. People may experience extreme pleasure and joy from activities and be hyperactive. They may also talk rapidly due to having many ideas at once. (**Mood disorder episodes**)

3. A mixed episode is characterized by the symptoms of both manic and major depressive episodes occurring every day for at least one week. (**Mood disorder episodes**)

4. Electroconvulsive therapy (ECT) is a biological treatment for severe depression that involves applying electrical impulses throughout the brain to produce seizures. (**Mood disorder episodes**)

5. Major depressive disorder is a mood disorder involving one or more major depressive episodes. (**Major depressive disorder**)

6. Dysthymic disorder is a mood disorder involving a persistently depressed mood, low self-esteem, withdrawal, and pessimism that is present for at least two years. (**Dysthymic disorder**)

7. Cyclothymic disorder is a chronic mood disorder which involves alternating mood elevation and depression which are less severe than major depressive or manic episodes. (**Cyclothymic disorder**)

8. **False.** When diagnosing a major depressive episode, clinicians should *not* ignore symptoms that are cultural norms. (**Mood disorder episodes**)

9. **True.** In elderly adults, cognitive symptoms may be the most prominent in a major depressive episode. (**Major depressive disorder**)

10. **True.** Mixed episodes are more in common in younger individuals and in males than in females. (**Mood disorder episodes**)

11. **False.** Prevalence rates for major depressive disorder are *unrelated* to ethnicity, education, income, or marital status. (**Major depressive disorder**)

12. **True.** In major depression, preadolescent boys and girls are equally affected. (**Major depressive disorder**)

13. **True.** In bipolar I disorder, the first episode is more likely to be a manic episode in males and a depressive episode in females. (**Bipolar disorders**)

14. A major depressive episode is characterized by a two-week period of depressed mood or loss of interest in most activities. Children and adolescents may be irritable. The person will also experience several other symptoms (at least four) including changes in appetite, changes in sleep, changes in activity level, loss of energy, feeling worthless, trouble concentrating, and suicidal thoughts. (**Mood disorder episodes**)

15. Women report deepening depressive symptoms several days prior to menstruation. Depressive episodes are believed to occur twice as frequently in women than men. (**Mood disorder episodes**)

16. Manic episodes are identified by at least one week of elevated or expansive mood. There will also be inflated self-esteem, distractibility, decreased need for sleep, flight of ideas and rapid speech. (**Mood disorder episodes**)

17. A mixed episode is characterized by meeting the criteria for both a manic and a major depressive episode. The individual experiences alternating moods accompanied by symptoms of both manic and depressive episodes. Symptoms frequently include agitation, insomnia, appetite changes, psychotic features, and suicidal thinking. (**Mood disorder episodes**)

18. In adolescents, hypomanic episodes may be associated with school truancy, antisocial behavior, school failure, or substance use. (**Mood disorder episodes**)

19. This disorder is characterized by one or more major depressive episodes without a history of manic, mixed, or hypomanic episodes. (**Major depressive disorder**)

20. Major depressive disorder is twice as common in adolescent and adult females as in adolescent and adult males. However, in preadolescent children, boys and girls are equally affected. Rates in men and women are highest in the 25 to 44 year age group, whereas rates are lower for both men and women over age 65. (**Major depressive disorder**)

21. Dysthymic disorder is chronic depression that is continual in nature. Additional symptoms may include poor appetite, overeating, insomnia or sleeping excessively, low energy, low self-esteem, and feelings of hopelessness. Dysthymic disorder is less severe than depression but chronic in nature. (**Dysthymic disorder**)

22. The main symptom of bipolar I disorder is the occurrence of one or more manic or mixed episodes. Often individuals have also had one or more major depressive episodes. (**Bipolar disorders**)

23. The main symptom of bipolar II disorder is the occurrence of one or more major depressive episodes and at least one hypomanic episode. (**Bipolar disorders**)

24. The essential symptom of cyclothymic disorder is a chronic, fluctuating mood involving periods of hypomanic symptoms and depressive symptoms. The person may be regarded as temperamental, moody, unpredictable, inconsistent, or unreliable. Cyclothymia is less severe than bipolar I disorder but chronic in nature. (**Cyclothymic disorder**)

25. Most evidence suggests that mood disorders have a genetic component and run in families. This may be the result of many genes having an additive effect. This may be a vulnerability to develop depression in response to stressful life events. Stressful events may also affect our hormones, which in turn affect neurotransmitter systems, especially serotonin and norepinephrine. There may also be a psychological vulnerability experienced by some as feeling inadequate in dealing with life. This psychological vulnerability may enhance the severity of our responses to stress. (**Mood disorders etiology and treatment**)

26. There are both biological treatments and psychological treatments for mood disorders. The biological treatments include medications and electroconvulsive therapy (ECT). There are three types of antidepressants used to treat depression: tricyclics, monoamine oxidase (MAO) inhibitors, and selective serotonergic reuptake inhibitors (SSRI's). Tricyclic antidepressants are the most common and have been found to relieve symptoms in 50 percent of patients. Tricyclics work by blocking the reuptake of norepinephrine. However, tricyclics can be lethal, so care must be exercised when prescribing these to suicidal patients. MAO inhibitors are as effective as tricyclics and work by blocking the enzyme that

breaks down norepinephrine and serotonin. MAO inhibitors are used less often because of serious side effects. SSRI's work by blocking the reuptake of serotonin, the best known of which is Prozac. The effectiveness of all of these drug treatments is similar. (**Mood disorders etiology and treatment**)

27. Yes, another antimanic drug with equal effectiveness, called lithium, is used to treat bipolar disorder. Lithium is a salt found naturally. The dosage of lithium must be carefully regulated to prevent poisoning or thyroid problems. (**Mood disorders etiology and treatment**)

28. Electroconvulsive therapy (ECT) is a biological treatment for severe depression. It involves applying electrical impulses throughout the brain to produce seizures. It can be an effective treatment for severe depression for those unresponsive to medication or other treatments. About 50 percent to 70 percent of patients not responding to medication can benefit from ECT. (**Mood disorders etiology and treatment**)

29. Cognitive therapy and interpersonal therapy are the two most effective psychological treatments. Cognitive therapy involves identifying and modifying negative thoughts related to mood disorders. These thoughts are replaced with more positive beliefs and attitudes, which usually leads to more adaptive behavior and better coping styles. Interpersonal psychotherapy is a brief treatment that emphasizes resolving interpersonal problems. Interpersonal problems and stresses are resolved and the client is taught new skills that will help him or her form new interpersonal relationships. (**Mood disorders etiology and treatment**)

30. Schneidman pioneered the research on suicidal risk factors. One such factor is a family history of suicide. Another risk factor is having low serotonin levels, which are associated with impulsivity and instability. Additionally, over 90 percent of those who commit suicide suffer from a psychological disorder. Suicide is often associated with mood disorders, as many as 60 percent of suicides have a mood disorder. Alcohol use and abuse is associated with 25 percent to 50 percent of suicides. Yet another risk factor is a past history of suicide attempts. One other risk factor is a severe, stressful event that is perceived as shameful or humiliating. (**Suicide**)

31. No. Most clusters of suicides occur among adolescents, with as many as 5 percent of all adolescent suicides representing "copycat" suicides. (**Suicide**)

Grade Yourself

Circle the numbers of the questions you missed, then fill in the total incorrect for each topic. If you answered more than three questions incorrectly, you need to focus on that topic. (If a topic has fewer than three questions and you had at least one wrong, we suggest you study that topic also. Read your textbook or a review book, or ask your teacher for help.)

Subject: Mood Disorders

Topic	Question Numbers	Number Incorrect
Mood disorder episodes	1, 2, 3, 4, 5, 8, 10, 13, 16, 17, 18	
Major depressive disorder	5, 9, 11, 12, 14, 15, 19, 20	
Dysthymic disorder	6, 21	
Cyclothymic disorder	7, 24	
Bipolar disorders	13, 22, 23	
Mood disorders etiology and treatment	25, 26, 27, 28, 29	
Suicide	30, 31	

Sleep Disorders

Brief Yourself

Roughly one-third of each day is spent sleeping. Most of us think that eight hours of sleep per night is normal, but normal sleeping patterns are subject to great personal variation. We all probably know someone who has a problem sleeping. Sleep disorders are organized into two major categories: *dyssomnias* and *parasomnias*. Dyssomnias involve problems in getting to sleep or getting sufficient high-quality sleep. Parasomnias are typified by abnormal behavior or physiological events that occur during sleep. Examples of parasomnias are nightmares and sleepwalking.

Test Yourself

Define the terms in questions 1–7.

1. Dyssomnias

2. Parasomnias

3. Insomnia

4. Hypersomnia

5. Kleine-Levin syndrome

6. Narcolepsy

7. Cataplexy

Questions 8–15 are true-false.

8. Survey data demonstrate that complaints of insomnia are most prevalent with increasing age and among males.

9. The main characteristic of primary hypersomnia is excessive sleepiness for at least one month.

10. Kleine-Levin syndrome affects males about three times more often than it affects females.

11. Sleep apnea involves repeated irresistible attacks of refreshing sleep, cataplexy, and recurrent intrusions of elements of rapid eye movement sleep into the transition period between sleep and wakefulness.

12. Recurrent primary hypersomnia involves indiscriminate sexuality and compulsive overeating.

13. In young children, the signs and symptoms of breathing-related sleep disorder are more subtle than those in adults and the diagnosis is more difficult to establish.

14. Eastward travel is typically more difficult for most individuals to tolerate than westward travel.

15. Nightmare disorder is least likely to appear in children exposed to severe psychosocial stressors.

16. What are dyssomnias?

17. What is primary insomnia?

18. Describe primary hypersomnia.

19. What is recurrent primary hypersomnia?

20. Which gender is affected more by Kleine-Levin syndrome?

21. What is narcolepsy?

22. What is a breathing-related sleep disorder?

23. What kind of breathing-related sleep disorder is more common among middle-aged adults?

24. Describe circadian rhythm sleep disorder.

25. What are the subtypes of circadian rhythm sleep disorder?

26. What are parasomnias?

27. What is nightmare disorder?

28. How common is nightmare disorder?

29. Describe sleep terror disorder.

30. How common is sleep terror disorder?

31. What is sleepwalking disorder?

32. How common is sleepwalking disorder?

Check Yourself

1. Dyssomnias involve problems in getting to sleep or getting sufficient high-quality sleep. (**Dyssomnias**)

2. Parasomnias are typified by abnormal behavior or physiological events that occur during sleep. (**Parasomnias**)

3. Primary insomnia involves complaints of trouble getting to sleep, maintaining sleep, or not feeling rested after sleep. (**Dyssomnias**)

4. Hypersomnia is excessive sleepiness for at least one month as evidenced either by prolonged sleep episodes or by daytime sleep episodes occurring almost daily. (**Dyssomnias**)

5. In the recurrent form of primary hypersomnia known as Kleine-Levin syndrome, individuals may spend 18–20 hours asleep or in bed. (**Dyssomnias**)

6. Narcolepsy is typified by repeated irresistible attacks of refreshing sleep and recurrent intrusions of elements of rapid eye movement (REM) sleep into the transition period between sleep and wakefulness. (**Dyssomnias**)

7. Cataplexy is a brief loss of muscle tone experienced during narcolepsy. (**Dyssomnias**)

8. **False.** Survey data demonstrate that complaints of insomnia are most prevalent with increasing age and among *women*. (**Dyssomnias**)

9. **True.** The main characteristic of primary hypersomnia is excessive sleepiness for at least one month. (**Dyssomnias**)

10. **True.** Kleine-Levin syndrome affects males about three times more often than it affects females. (**Dyssomnias**)

11. **False.** *Narcolepsy* involves repeated irresistible attacks of refreshing sleep, cataplexy, and recurrent intrusions of elements of rapid eye movement sleep into the transition period between sleep and wakefulness. (**Dyssomnias**)

12. **True.** Recurrent primary hypersomnia involves indiscriminate sexuality and compulsive overeating. (**Dyssomnias**)

13. **True.** In young children, the signs and symptoms of breathing-related sleep disorder are more subtle than those in adults and the diagnosis is more difficult to establish. (**Dyssomnias**)

14. **True.** Eastward travel is typically more difficult for most individuals to tolerate than westward travel. (**Dyssomnias**)

15. **False.** Nightmare disorder is *most* likely to appear in children exposed to severe psychosocial stressors. (**Parasomnias**)

16. Dyssomnias are disorders of initiating or maintaining sleep or of excessive sleepiness and are typified by a disturbance in the amount, quality, or timing of sleep. This includes primary insomnia, primary

hypersomnia, narcolepsy, breathing-related sleep disorders, and circadian rhythm sleep disorder. **(Dyssomnias)**

17. Primary insomnia consists of trouble getting to sleep, trouble maintaining sleep, or not feeling rested after sleep, that lasts for at least one month. **(Dyssomnias)**

18. Primary hypersomnia is excessive sleepiness for at least one month as indicated by prolonged sleep episodes or by daytime sleep episodes. The excessive sleepiness must be sufficiently severe to cause distress or impairment in social, occupational, or other important areas of functioning. **(Dyssomnias)**

19. Recurrent means that there are periods of excessive sleepiness that last at least three days and occur several times a year for at least two years. Most individuals with primary hypersomnia have consistent and persistent symptoms. In the recurrent form of primary hypersomnia known as Kleine-Levin syndrome, individuals may spend 18–20 hours asleep. Indiscriminate sexuality, including inappropriate sexual advances and overt masturbation, can be seen in males (and less often in females). Compulsive overeating with acute weight gain may occur. Irritability, depression, confusion, and occasional hallucinations have been described in some individuals. **(Dyssomnias)**

20 . Kleine-Levin syndrome affects males about three times more often than it affects females. **(Dyssomnias)**

21. Narcolepsy consists of irresistible attacks of sleep, cataplexy, and recurrent intrusions of rapid eye movement (REM) sleep into the transition period between sleep and wakefulness. The individual's sleepiness typically decreases after a sleep attack, only to return several hours later. **(Dyssomnias)**

22. The essential feature of breathing-related sleep disorder is sleep disruption, leading to excessive sleepiness in insomnia, that is judged to be due to abnormalities of ventilation during sleep (e.g., sleep apnea or central alveolar hypoventilation). **(Dyssomnias)**

23. The obstructive sleep apnea syndrome is most common in middle-aged, overweight males and preadolescent children with enlarged tonsils. The central alveolar hypoventilation syndrome is more common in obese young-adult males. Aging leads to an increase in the frequency of both obstructive and central apnea events. **(Dyssomnias)**

24. Circadian rhythm sleep disorder involves a pattern of sleep disruption that results from a mismatch between the individual's internal sleep-wake system and environmental demands regarding the timing and duration of sleep. Individuals with this disorder may complain of insomnia at certain times during the day and excessive sleepiness at other times, with resulting impairment in social, occupational, or other important areas of functioning or marked subjective distress. **(Dyssomnias)**

25. The delayed sleep phase type of circadian rhythm sleep disorder results from an internal sleep-wake cycle that is delayed relative to the demands of society. These individuals are "locked in" to habitually late sleep hours and cannot move these sleep hours forward to an earlier time. In the jet lag type of circadian rhythm sleep disorder, the disturbance arises from conflict between the pattern of sleep and wakefulness required by a new time zone. The severity of the jet lag type is related to the number of time zones traveled through, with the most difficulties noted after traveling eight or more time zones in less than 24 hours. Eastward travel is more difficult for most individuals to tolerate than westward travel. In the shift work type of circadian rhythm sleep disorder, the disturbance comes from conflict between the pattern of sleep and wakefulness generated by the circadian system and the desired pattern of sleep required by shift work. Rotating-shift schedules are the most disruptive because they force sleep and wakefulness into aberrant circadian positions and prevent any consistent adjustment. **(Dyssomnias)**

26. Parasomnias are disorders characterized by abnormal behavior or physiological events occurring in association with sleep. In particular, these disorders involve activation of the autonomic nervous system, motor system, or cognitive processes during sleep or sleep-wake transitions. Different parasomnias occur at different times during sleep. **(Parasomnias)**

27. The main characteristic of nightmare disorder is the persistent occurrence of frightening dreams that lead to waking up from sleep. The individual becomes fully alert on awakening. **(Parasomnias)**

28. Between 10 percent and 50 percent of children ages 3 to 5 years have nightmares of sufficient intensity to disturb their parents. In the adult population, as many as 50 percent of individuals may report at least an occasional nightmare. However, the actual prevalence of nightmare disorder is unknown. **(Parasomnias)**

29. Sleep terror disorder is the reported occurrence of abrupt waking up from sleep usually beginning with a panicky scream or cry. Sleep terrors usually begin during the first third of the major sleep episode and last 1 to 10 minutes. The episodes are accompanied by arousal of intense fear. During an episode, the individual is difficult to awaken or comfort. If the individual awakens after the sleep terror, no dream is recalled or only fragmentary, single images are recalled. On awakening the following morning, the individual has amnesia for the event. Sleep terrors are also called "night terrors" or *pavor nocturnus*. **(Parasomnias)**

30. The prevalence of sleep terror episodes has been estimated at 1 percent to 6 percent among children and at less than 1 percent of adults. **(Parasomnias)**

31. Sleepwalking disorder refers to repeated episodes of complex motor behavior during sleep, including rising from bed and walking about. Sleepwalking episodes begin during slow-wave sleep and therefore most often occur during the first third of the night. During episodes, the individual has reduced alertness and responsiveness and relative unresponsiveness to communication with others or efforts to be awakened by others. The individual has limited recall for the events of the episode. **(Parasomnias)**

32. Between 10 percent and 30 of children have had at least one episode of sleepwalking, but the prevalence of sleepwalking disorder is much lower. Sleepwalking disorder occurs with equal frequency in both sexes. **(Parasomnias)**

Grade Yourself

Circle the numbers of the questions you missed, then fill in the total incorrect for each topic. If you answered more than three questions incorrectly, you need to focus on that topic. (If a topic has fewer than three questions and you had at least one wrong, we suggest you study that topic also. Read your textbook or a review book, or ask your teacher for help.)

Subject: Sleep Disorders

Topic	Question Numbers	Number Incorrect
Dyssomnias	1, 3, 4, 5, 6, 7, 8, 9, 10, 11, 12, 13, 14, 16, 17, 18, 19, 20, 21, 22, 23, 24, 25	
Parasomnias	2, 15, 26, 27, 28, 29, 30, 31, 32	

Personality Disorders

13

Brief Yourself

Personality disorders are long-lasting patterns of behaving and relating to oneself and others that are maladaptive, and cause distress and functional impairment. They are considered chronic, meaning they endure over a long time period, rather than coming and going as many other disorders. They are thought to begin in childhood and last throughout one's lifetime. The person with the disorder may in fact feel no distress, however, the distress may be felt by those affected by this person's actions. There are 10 personality disorders, all of which are diagnosed on Axis II of the DSM-IV system. Personality disorders are classified according to three clusters: A, B, and C. Cluster A is referred to as the "odd" or "eccentric" cluster and includes the paranoid, schizoid and schizotypal personality disorders. Cluster B is referred to as the "dramatic" or "emotional" cluster; it includes the antisocial, borderline, histrionic and narcissistic personality disorders. Cluster C is referred to as the "anxious" or "fearful" cluster. This cluster includes the avoidant, dependent and obsessive-compulsive personality disorders.

Test Yourself

Define the terms in questions 1–4.

1. Personality disorder

2. Cluster A

3. Cluster B

4. Cluster C

Questions 5–14 are true-false.

5. Cluster C is referred to as the "dramatic" or "emotional" cluster; it includes the antisocial, borderline, histrionic and narcissistic personality disorders.

6. Women comprise about three-fourths of the cases of borderline personality disorder.

7. People with paranoid personality disorder are distrustful and suspicious of other people.

8. People with schizoid personality disorder prefer solitary activities and may be perceived as self-absorbed.

9. People with schizoid personality disorder have odd beliefs about possessing magical powers and psychic ability.

10. Antisocial personality disorder is viewed as the model for psychopathy, sociopathy, or dissocial personality disorders.

11. People with antisocial personality disorder tend to come from families of high socioeconomic status.

12. People with borderline personality disorder tend to engage in relationships that are usually unstable, falling in love quickly and rushing through the relationship.

13. Of those diagnosed with narcissistic personality disorder, 10 percent to 25 percent are male.

14. Individuals with avoidant personality disorder are best characterized as people who look for others to take care of them.

15. How common are personality disorders?

16. How many personality disorders are there?

17. What are the three clusters of personality disorders?

18. Do some personality disorders occur more often in men or women?

19. Describe the paranoid personality disorder.

20. What is schizoid personality disorder?

21. Describe schizotypal personality disorder.

22. When is the onset of schizotypal personality disorder?

23. What is antisocial personality disorder?

24. How common is antisocial personality disorder?

25. Describe borderline personality disorder.

26. What is histrionic personality disorder?

27. Describe narcissistic personality disorder.

28. Is there any one group more likely to suffer from narcissistic personality disorder?

29. Describe avoidant personality disorder.

30. When is the onset of avoidant personality disorder?

31. How common is avoidant personality disorder?

32. What is dependent personality disorder?

33. Describe obsessive-compulsive personality disorder.

34. Can personality disorders be treated?

 # Check Yourself

1. Personality disorders are long-lasting patterns of behaving and relating to oneself and others that are maladaptive and cause distress and functional impairment. (**Defining personality disorders**)

2. Cluster A is referred to as the "odd" or "eccentric" cluster and includes the paranoid, schizoid and schizotypal personality disorders. (**Cluster A**)

3. Cluster B is referred to as the "dramatic" or "emotional" cluster; it includes the antisocial, borderline, histrionic and narcissistic personality disorders. (**Cluster B**)

4. Cluster C is referred to as the "anxious" or "fearful" cluster. This cluster includes the avoidant, dependent and obsessive-compulsive personality disorders. (**Cluster C**)

5. **False.** Cluster *B* is referred to as the "dramatic" or "emotional" cluster; it includes the antisocial, borderline, histrionic and narcissistic personality disorders. (**Cluster A**)

6. **True.** Women comprise about three-fourths of the cases of borderline personality disorder. (**Cluster B**)

7. **True.** People with paranoid personality disorder are distrustful and suspicious of other people. (**Cluster A**)

8. **True.** People with schizoid personality disorder prefer solitary activities and may be perceived as self-absorbed. (**Cluster A**)

9. **False.** People with *schizotypal* personality disorder have odd beliefs about possessing magical powers and psychic ability. (**Cluster A**)

10. **True.** Antisocial personality disorder is viewed as the model for psychopathy, sociopathy, or dissocial personality disorders. (**Cluster B**)

11. **False.** People with antisocial personality disorder tend to come from families of *low* socioeconomic status. (**Cluster B**)

12. **True.** People with borderline personality disorder tend to engage in relationships that are usually unstable, falling in love quickly and rushing through the relationship. (**Cluster B**)

13. **False.** Of those diagnosed with narcissistic personality disorder, 50 percent to 75 percent are male. (**Cluster C**)

14. **False.** Individuals with dependent personality disorder are best characterized as people who look for others to take care of them. (**Cluster C**)

15. It is estimated that between 10 percent and 13 percent of the general population suffers from personality disorders, so that means that it is more common than many other disorders. (**Defining personality disorders**)

16. There are 10 personality disorders, all of which are diagnosed on Axis II of the DSM-IV system. (**Defining personality disorders**)

17. Personality disorders are classified according to three clusters: A, B, and C. Cluster A is referred to as the "odd" or "eccentric" cluster and includes the paranoid, schizoid and schizotypal personality disorders. Cluster B is referred to as the "dramatic" or "emotional" cluster; it includes the antisocial, borderline, histrionic and narcissistic personality disorders. Cluster C is referred to as the "anxious" or "fearful" cluster. This cluster includes the avoidant, dependent and obsessive-compulsive personality disorders. (**Defining personality disorders**)

18. Yes, historically, the histrionic and dependent personality disorders have been found to occur more often in women than men. However, most other personality disorders except borderline occur more often in men than women. Borderline personality disorder is diagnosed more among women. Women comprise about three-fourths of the cases of borderline personality disorder. (**Defining personality disorders**)

19. People with paranoid personality disorder are distrustful and suspicious of other people and typically want to harm others. This disorder usually begins in early adulthood. Many people who suffer from this disorder usually believe that people will harm and deceive them. They think that other people are planning to hurt them and will react against them, as a "pre-emptive strike," without a good reason. They also doubt the

loyalty of others and will not even trust their friends or colleagues. These individuals are unwilling to share secrets with friends or other people, because they are afraid these secrets will be used against them. They may misinterpret compliments and they do not let others help them if they are having problems. These individuals find it hard to forgive others and become very hostile, since they are quickly angered when insulted. They are jealous and may think that their spouse or partner is unfaithful. **(Cluster A)**

20. Schizoid personality disorder is another Cluster A disorder, which is characterized by a constant pattern of social detachment and low emotionality in interpersonal relationships. These persons prefer to be alone and are often labeled "loners." They do not develop close relationships and lack intimacy in relationships. Individuals prefer solitary activities and may be perceived as self-absorbed. They rarely experience strong emotions such as anger and happiness. When in stressful situations, they may have brief psychotic episodes. When they do reveal something about themselves, they feel uncomfortable and it is a painful experience. **(Cluster A)**

21. The main characteristic of schizotypal personality disorder is a pattern of problems with social relationships, in addition to cognitive delusions and distorted behavior. These individuals may erroneously interpret situations and are superstitious. They have odd beliefs about possessing magical powers and psychic ability. Their speech is unusual, vague and loose. Interpersonal relationships are affected because others' cues are misread and situations are reacted to differently. The person may feel uncomfortable in dealing with interpersonal relationships. They are unhappy about their lack of social interaction and close relationships yet do not want to get intimately involved. Anxiety is very common among people with this disorder, and it may come from a distrust of people. In response to this stress, individuals may experience transient psychotic episodes. Over half of all people effected by this disorder have had at least one major depressive episode. **(Cluster A)**

22. Schizotypal personality disorder may be first noted in children and adolescents with poor relationships with peers, social anxiety, and strange thoughts and feelings. **(Cluster A)**

23. Antisocial personality disorder is a Cluster B disorder, typified by a pervasive pattern of disregard for and violation of the rights of others which usually begins in childhood or early adolescence and continues to into adulthood. Antisocial personality disorder is seen as a model for psychopathy, sociopathy, or dissocial personality disorder. These persons tend to be very manipulative and deceiving. In order to be diagnosed with antisocial personality disorder, the person would be 18 years of age and have had conduct disorder prior to age 15. These individuals tend to be very aggressive towards people and animals, engage in property destruction, are dishonest and violate the law. They do not care about the feelings of other people. They may lie very well. They are also impulsive, making decisions without considering the consequences. These individuals are also irresponsible, they cannot keep a job and have financial difficulties. **(Cluster B)**

24. Studies indicate that the prevalence of antisocial personality disorder in males is 3 percent and females is 1 percent. In clinical settings, the rates range from 3 percent to 30 percent. Men tend to suffer from this disorder more than women. Many women who have a conduct disorder and display aggressive behavior might be diagnosed as having antisocial personality disorder. **(Cluster B)**

25. These individuals are best characterized as having a general pattern of unstable relationships, self-esteem, and emotions and unpredictable behaviors that usually begin in early adulthood and are found across many settings. These individuals have a fear of abandonment. They may overreact to different situations in their environment. They also tend to engage in relationships that are usually unstable, falling in love quickly and rushing through the relationship. An individual with this disorder usually has problems with his or her self-image, with fluctuations in self-confidence. They are also impulsive, doing things without thinking about consequences, engaging in reckless behavior such as gambling, financial irresponsibility, substance abuse

and unsafe sex. They may want to hurt themselves, making suicide a possibility. Individuals with this disorder often change moods, have persistent feelings of loneliness, have difficulty with anger management, and having feelings of paranoia or dissociation; these typically follow stressful situations. **(Cluster B)**

26. The main symptom of histrionic personality disorder is pervasive and excessive emotionality and attention-seeking behavior. This behavior begins by early adulthood and is present across many situations. Individuals with histrionic personality disorder are feel uncomfortable or unappreciated when they are not the center of attention. They draw attention to themselves and may charm new acquaintances by their enthusiasm, openness, or flirtatiousness. If they are not the center of attention, they may do something dramatic to focus attention on themselves. Their appearance and behavior are often inappropriately sexual and are directed at many nonromantic relationships. They use physical appearance to draw attention to themselves and are concerned with impressing others. Their speech is excessively impressionistic and lacking in detail. Individuals with this disorder are characterized by theatricality and a exaggerated emotional expression. These individuals are highly suggestible and are easily influenced by others. **(Cluster B)**

27. Narcissistic personality disorder is the last Cluster B disorder and is typified by grandiosity, need for admiration, and lack of empathy. This disorder typically begins by early adulthood. This person should have at least five of the following criteria. The first criterion is an egotistic sense of self-importance; frequently overexaggerating their accomplishments and assuming that others place the same value on these accomplishments. The second criterion is a preoccupation with unlimited success, power, intelligence, and attractiveness, comparing themselves with famous or successful people. The third criterion is that these individuals believe that they are unique and superior to others. Fourth, these individuals have a fragile self-esteem that requires a great deal of admiration. A fifth criterion is that they have unreasonable expectations of favorable treatment and become annoyed if they are not catered to. The sixth criterion is the conscious and sometimes unconscious exploitation of others. Another criterion is a lack of empathy and difficulty recognizing the feelings of others. Moreover, they believe that others are envious of them because of their success and perfection. Last, they are boastful and snobbish and patronize others. **(Cluster B)**

28. Of those diagnosed with narcissistic personality disorder, 50 percent to 75 percent are male. Although many teens may seem to have narcissistic traits, it does not mean that they may later develop this disorder. There is no specific culture or age group where this disorder is common, but it does develop in early adulthood. **(Cluster B)**

29. Avoidant personality disorder is characterized by hypersensitivity to negative evaluation, social inhibitions, and feelings of inadequacy. The individual in question must have at least four of the diagnostic criteria. First, these individuals fear criticism and rejection, so they avoid work or school activities that require social interaction. Second, they avoid making new friends unless there is certainty that the friends will like them. Third, these individuals fear being exposed and ashamed, so they have trouble talking about themselves and sharing feelings. Fourth, they are preoccupied with social criticism and rejection. Fifth, these individuals are inhibited in social situations involving strangers because they have a low self-esteem and feel inadequate. Sixth, they feel inferior to others and that they are personally unappealing. Last, these individuals are reluctant to take personal risks because of possible embarrassment. This results in an extremely restricted lifestyle. **(Cluster C)**

30. The onset of avoidant personality disorder is usually in adulthood and one should be careful in misdiagnosing children or adolescents that may have some of the avoidant traits. **(Cluster C)**

31. In the general population, the prevalence of this disorder is low, from .5 percent to 1 percent. Approximately 10 percent of outpatients seen in mental health clinics are reported as having this disorder. **(Cluster C)**

32. Individuals who have dependent personality disorder are best characterized as people who look for others to take care of them. They tend to be compliant and clinging in order to avoid separation. They are indecisive, passive and avoid responsibility in most areas of their life. Adults may still need help from their parents in making life decisions, whereas adolescents may permit their parents to decide for them such things as what to wear, where to go, and who to have as friends. This disorder can be found in individuals with medical conditions, but the avoidance of responsibility goes beyond what is expected. They usually agree with others in order to avoid conflict and possible abandonment. They have problems starting tasks or doing things on their own. They feel awkward alone so they tend to "hang around" with others even if they do not like who they are with. Because dependent individuals do not like to be alone, when a relationship ends, they usually seek out another in order to avoid the fear of having to take care of themselves. **(Cluster C)**

33. Obsessive-compulsive peronality disorder (OCD) is a Cluster C disorder in which a person is fixated on orderliness, perfectionism, and control at the expense of flexibility and efficiency. A preoccupation with details prevents them from completing tasks. **(Cluster C)**

34. Yes, however, the prognoses and outcome for these disorders are usually poor. Personality disorders may also interfere with treatment of coexisting Axis I disorders. **(Treatment)**

Grade Yourself

Circle the numbers of the questions you missed, then fill in the total incorrect for each topic. If you answered more than three questions incorrectly, you need to focus on that topic. (If a topic has fewer than three questions and you had at least one wrong, we suggest you study that topic also. Read your textbook or a review book, or ask your teacher for help.)

Subject: Personality Disorders

Topic	Question Numbers	Number Incorrect
Defining personality disorders	1, 15, 16, 17, 18	
Cluster A	2, 5, 7, 8, 9, 19, 20, 21, 22, , 29	
Cluster B	3, 6, 10, 11, 12, 23, 24, 25, 26, 27, 28	
Cluster C	4, 13, 14, 29, 30, 31, 32, 33	
Treatment	34	

Substance-Related Disorders

14

Brief Yourself

Substance-related disorders cover the range of problems encountered when someone uses or abuses drugs. *Psychoactive* drugs are substances that alter the way people think, feel and act. These are drugs such as alcohol, cocaine, heroin, marijuana, etc. Some of these substances are illicit and some are not. Legal drugs include alcohol, nicotine, and caffeine. Illicit substances include heroin, cocaine, crack cocaine, PCP, marijuana, and inhalants. The use of such substances is costly in human and economic terms. There are also those who use many substances, which is called *polydrug* or *polysubstance* use. This chapter will discuss the differences between abuse, intoxication and dependence. Additionally, drug withdrawal is examined. Drugs are typically classified according to their effects on the human nervous system: depressants, stimulants, hallucinogens and opiates. Some drugs, like marijuana, do not fit into any single category.

Test Yourself

Define the terms in questions 1–16.

1. Psychoactive substances

2. Polysubstance use

3. Intoxication

4. Dependence

5. Abuse

6. Withdrawal

7. Tolerance

8. Depressants

9. Stimulants

10. Hallucinogens

11. Opiates

12. Cannabis

13. Dementia

14. Wernicke's disease

15. Withdrawal delirium

16. Fetal alcohol syndrome

Questions 17–24 are true-false.

17. Intoxication is dependent upon the specific drug taken, the quantity of drug taken, and the person's biological reaction to this drug.

18. When drug use disrupts school, employment or relationships, then it is considered abuse.

19. Withdrawal symptoms can be alleviated with use of the same drug or a similar drug.

20. Caffeine, amphetamines, cocaine and nicotine are depressants.

21. Methadone is a synthetic hallucinogen.

22. It is recommended that alcohol be consumed by pregnant women.

23. Recent research shows only that babies of women who abuse alcohol while pregnant had decreased birth weight but no cognitive or motor deficits at birth or one month subsequent to birth.

24. Caffeine is believed to be the least harmful of all the addictive drugs.

25. What is intoxication?

26. Differentiate between substance abuse and substance dependence.

27. What is tolerance?

28. What is withdrawal?

29. How are drugs classified?

30. Describe depressants and give some examples.

31. What are stimulants?

32. Describe opiates.

33. What are hallucinogens?

34. What is marijuana?

35. Discuss alcohol-related disorders.

36. What do people who are alcohol dependent experience?

37. What are the long-term effects of heavy drinking?

38. Is a pregnant woman's consumption of alcohol dangerous to her fetus?

39. Discuss amphetamines.

40. Describe amphetamine intoxication.

41. Discuss cocaine.

42. Describe "crack babies."

43. How many people use cocaine?

44. Discuss nicotine-related disorders.

45. Describe caffeine-related disorders.

46. What is opioid intoxication?

47. Describe opioid withdrawal.

48. How many people use opiates?

49. Discuss cannabis-related disorders.

50. Discuss LSD.

51. What causes substance-related disorders?

52. How are substance-related disorders treated?

Check Yourself

1. Psychoactive drugs are substances that alter the way people think, feel and act. (**Defining substance-related disorders**)

2. Polysubstance use refers to the use of many psychoactive substances or drugs. (**Defining substance-related disorders**)

3. Intoxication is a physiological reaction to the use of psychoactive substances that is sometimes referred to as "getting high" or being "drunk." (**Defining substance-related disorders**)

4. Substance dependence, also called "addiction," refers to a pattern of drug use typified by increased tolerance, withdrawal symptoms, unsuccessful efforts to quit, and expenditure of much effort in order to obtain the drug or recover from its effects. (**Defining substance-related disorders**)

5. The main criteria for determining abuse is how much the drug use interferes with the person's life. (**Defining substance-related disorders**)

6. Withdrawal is a severe negative physiological reaction to cessation of drug use. (**Defining substance-related disorders**)

7. Tolerance is the need for more and more of the drug in order to achieve the desired effect ("get high"). (**Defining substance-related disorders**)

8. Depressants decrease central nervous system activity resulting in a calming effect. (**Drug classification**)

9. Stimulants increase central nervous system activity, resulting in a more active and alert person. (**Drug classification**)

10. Hallucinogens produce delusions and hallucinations. They may also cause paranoia and alter your sensory perception. (**Drug classification**)

11. Opiates are naturally occurring chemicals in poppies that reduce pain and induce sleep. (**Drug classification**)

12. Cannabis is the hemp plant that marijuana comes from. (**Drug classification**)

13. Dementia refers to a general deficit in intellectual abilities resulting from alcohol poisoning the brain. (**Depressant disorders**)

14. Wernicke's disease is typified by confusion, loss of muscle coordination and unintelligible speech. (**Depressant disorders**)

15. Withdrawal delirium is manifested by severe body tremors and frightening hallucinations. (**Depressant disorders**)

16. Fetal alcohol syndrome is a combination of many problems, such as cognitive and behavior problems and learning difficulties, that appear in infants due to a mother's drinking during pregnancy. (**Depressant disorders**)

17. **True.** Intoxication is dependent upon the specific drug taken, the quantity of drug taken, and the person's biological reaction to this drug. (**Defining substance-related disorders**)

18. **True.** When drug use disrupts school, employment or relationships, then it is considered abuse. (**Defining substance-related disorders**)

19. **True.** Withdrawal symptoms can be alleviated with use of the same drug or a similar drug. (**Defining substance-related disorders**)

20. **False.** Caffeine, amphetamines, cocaine and nicotine are *stimulants*. (**Drug classification**)

21. **False.** Methadone is a synthetic *opiate*. (**Drug classification**)

22. **False.** It is recommended that *no* alcohol be consumed by pregnant women. (**Depressant disorders**)

23. **True.** Recent research shows only that these babies had decreased birth weight but no cognitive or motor deficits at birth or one month subsequent to birth. (**Stimulant disorders**)

24. **True.** Caffeine is believed to be the least harmful of all the addictive drugs. (**Stimulant disorders**)

25. It is a physiological reaction to the use of psychoactive substances that is sometimes referred to as "getting high" or being "drunk". In a state of intoxication, a person's judgment is impaired as well as motor coordination. There may also be emotional changes experienced by the user. Intoxication is dependent upon the specific drug taken, the quantity of drug taken, and the person's biological reaction to this drug. (**Defining substance-related disorders**)

26. Substance abuse refers to a pattern of drug use that causes distress or functional impairment. The main criteria for determining abuse is how much the drug use interferes with the person's life. When the use disrupts school, employment or relationships, then it is considered abuse. Substance dependence, also called "addiction," refers to a pattern of drug use typified by increased tolerance, withdrawal symptoms, unsuccessful efforts to quit, and expenditure of much effort in order to obtain the drug or recover from its effects. (**Defining substance-related disorders**)

27. It is the need for more and more of the drug in order to achieve the desired effect ("get high"). Using the same amount does not result in the desired effect. (**Defining substance-related disorders**)

28. Withdrawal is a severe negative physiological reaction to cessation of drug use. The symptoms can be alleviated with use of the same drug or a similar drug. (**Defining substance-related disorders**)

29. Typically drugs are classified according to the drug's effect on the central nervous system. There are four categories of psychoactive substances: depressants, stimulants, opiates, and hallucinogens. (**Drug classification**)

30. Depressants decrease central nervous system activity resulting in a calming effect. Drugs used as sedatives fall into this category, such as barbiturates and benzodiazepines (Valium). Alcohol is also a depressant. (**Drug classification**)

31. Stimulants increase central nervous system activity, resulting in a more active and alert person. Stimulants can also elevate mood. Caffeine and nicotine are stimulants, as are amphetamines and cocaine. Stimulants are the most commonly consumed drug in this country. (**Drug classification**)

32. Opiates are naturally occurring chemicals in poppies that reduce pain and induce sleep. Opiates are heroin, morphine, opium, and codeine. Synthetic types include methadone. (**Drug classification**)

33. Hallucinogens produce delusions and hallucinations. They may also cause paranoia and alter the user's sensory perception. Examples of hallucinogens are LSD, psilocybin and mescaline. (**Drug classification**)

34. Marijuana does not fit into any single category. Some label it as a hallucinogen because it may result in altered sensory experiences. (**Drug classification**)

35. Alcohol initially makes people feel more outgoing and less inhibited. When drinking continues, alcohol interferes with motor coordination and reaction time, slurs speech, and impairs decision-making ability. Alcohol affects many neurotransmitter systems in the body making it more difficult to study than other drugs. (**Depressant disorders**)

36. People may experience blackouts, seizures and hallucinations. These indicate brain damage has occurred. They may also develop dementia and Wernicke's disease. Dementia refers to a general deficit in intellectual abilities resulting from alcohol poisoning the brain. Wernicke's disease is typified by

confusion, loss of muscle coordination and unintelligible speech. This disease is believed to result from a thiamin deficiency (thiamin is poorly metabolized by heavy drinkers). (**Depressant disorders**)

37. Long-term drinking effects include hand tremors, vomiting, anxiety, hallucinations, and insomnia. This can lead to withdrawal delirium, which is manifested by severe body tremors and frightening hallucinations. (**Depressant disorders**)

38. Yes, it is recommended that no alcohol be consumed by a pregnant woman. When women drink during pregnancy, fetal alcohol syndrome (FAS) can result. This is a combination of many problems, such as cognitive and behavior problems and learning difficulties. Children born with FAS also have characteristic facial features including skin folds at the corner of the eye, small head circumference, small eye opening and thin upper lip. (**Depressant disorders**)

39. Amphetamines were first used as a treatment for asthma and nasal congestion. Now they are used to treat hypersomnia and narcolepsy. Amphetamines make people feel elated and reduce fatigue. Amphetamines are used by some to lose weight because they decrease your desire to eat. Amphetamines stimulate the central nervous system by increasing the activity of norepinephrine and dopamine. (**Stimulant disorders**)

40. Amphetamine intoxication may lead to social withdrawal, anxiety and anger. The person may also have hot and cold flashes, nausea and vomiting. Severe intoxication can cause hallucinations, panic, and paranoid delusions. (**Stimulant disorders**)

41. Cocaine is another stimulant derived from coca leaves. It is used as a local anesthetic. Cocaine replaced amphetamines as the main stimulant used in the 1970s. In small doses, cocaine increases alertness, a sense of euphoria and blood pressure. It also results in insomnia and loss of appetite. Cocaine makes the heart beat rapidly and irregularly, which can be fatal. Cocaine has effects similar to amphetamines on the brain. Cocaine makes more dopamine available which results in an "up" feeling. (**Stimulant disorders**)

42. Crack is a harder, rock-like form of cocaine. In the 1980s many children were born to crack-addicted mothers. These infants were believed to be more irritable, had high-pitched crying and were believed to be brain damaged. Recent research shows only that these babies had decreased birth weight but no cognitive or motor deficits at birth or one month subsequent to birth. Limited longitudinal evidence is available on this relatively new medical condition; several longitudinal studies are still in effect. (**Stimulant disorders**)

43. Cocaine use has decreased over the past 10 years, with less than 1 percent of Americans reporting cocaine use in 1994. (**Stimulant disorders**)

44. The nicotine found in cigarettes results in dependence, tolerance and withdrawal. Nicotine is a nervous system stimulant that relieves stress and elevates mood. It can also lead to high blood pressure and increase the risk of heart disease and cancer. High doses of nicotine can cause confusion, convulsions, and death. Smokers experience withdrawal symptoms when they are trying to quit, like irritability, anxiety, trouble concentrating, hunger and restlessness. (**Stimulant disorders**)

45. Caffeine is also a stimulant and is found in tea, coffee, chocolate, and colas. It is believed to be the least harmful of all the addictive drugs. Caffeine can elevate mood and decrease fatigue. In higher doses, it can cause insomnia. All people react differently to caffeine. Research suggests that moderate caffeine use by pregnant women does not harm developing fetuses. Regular caffeine use can lead to tolerance and withdrawal. Withdrawal symptoms include headaches, drowsiness and negative emotions. Caffeine affects the neurotransmitter adenosine. (**Stimulant disorders**)

46. Opiates create a feeling of euphoria, drowsiness and slow respiration. At higher doses, the slower breathing is much slower and can lead to death. (**Opiate disorders**)

47. Withdrawal from opiates can be very unpleasant; symptoms include excessive yawning, nausea, chills, muscle aches, diarrhea and insomnia. Symptoms appear 6 to 12 hours after cessation of drug, and the process may last a week. (**Opiate disorders**)

48. It is estimated that about one million people in the United States use opiates. Opiate use was more popular in the early 1970's and for the most part has been replaced by cocaine as the drug of choice. (**Opiate disorders**)

49. Marijuana was most popular in the 1960's and 1970's. It is still the most regularly used illicit drug in this country, with about five million people saying they use it at least weekly. Marijuana is the dried part of the hemp plant or cannabis. Cannabis intoxication can include mood swings, dreamlike states, and heightened sensory experiences. In larger doses, marijuana can lead to paranoia, hallucinations and dizziness. Chronic users may experience memory problems, low self-esteem, low motivation, and impaired relationships. Chronic users may report withdrawal symptoms that include irritability, restlessness, appetite loss, nausea and insomnia. (**Marijuana**)

50. LSD (lysergic acid diethylamide) is the most common hallucinogen. LSD intoxication includes intense sensory experiences and hallucinations. Tolerance to LSD can develop quickly. LSD loses its effectiveness if taken repeatedly for several days. Most hallucinogen users report no withdrawal symptoms. However, there may be side effects such as psychotic reactions, "bad trips," and paranoia. Hallucinogens resemble brain neurotransmitters chemically. LSD resembles serotonin, and mescaline resembles norepinephrine. (**Hallucinogen disorders**)

51. Exposure to and availability of drugs is necessary to become dependent upon drugs. This could come from family, friends, media, or other means of social influence. Cultural beliefs about drug use may also contribute to abuse. Some people use drugs without abusing them or becoming dependent upon them, so the link between use and abuse or dependence is complicated. Major stressors, genetic influences, and psychiatric conditions all may increase the risk for abuse or dependence. (**Etiology and treatment**)

52. The most efficacious drug treatment seems to be a combination of biological and psychosocial treatments. The biological treatments may prescribe drugs that substitute for the drug of abuse (like methadone treatment for opiate abuse). Psychosocial treatments may focus on controlling the use of drugs and preventing relapse once drug use is stopped. (**Etiology and treatment**)

Grade Yourself

Circle the numbers of the questions you missed, then fill in the total incorrect for each topic. If you answered more than three questions incorrectly, you need to focus on that topic. (If a topic has fewer than three questions and you had at least one wrong, we suggest you study that topic also. Read your textbook or a review book, or ask your teacher for help.)

Subject: Substance-Related Disorders

Topic	Question Numbers	Number Incorrect
Defining substance-related disorders	1, 2, 3, 4, 5, 6, 7, 17, 18, 19, 25, 26, 27, 28	
Drug classification	8, 9, 10, 11, 12, 20, 21, 29, 30, 31, 32, 33, 34	
Depressant disorders	13, 14, 15, 16, 22, 35, 36, 37, 38	
Stimulant disorders	23, 24, 39, 40, 41, 42, 43, 44, 45	
Opiate disorders	46, 47, 48	
Marijuana	49	
Hallucinogen disorders	50	
Etiology and treatment	51, 52	

Sexual Disorders

15

Brief Yourself

Sexual behaviors vary widely across cultures. In this country, prevailing views are quite tolerant of sexual variety until a sexual act results in distress or impaired functioning. When this occurs, one might be having a sexual disorder. There are three types of sexual disorders: *gender identity disorders*, *sexual dysfunctions* and *paraphilias*. *Gender identity disorder* refers to a dissatisfaction with one's biological sex. This disorder does not focus on behavior but rather on one's identity as male or female. *Sexual dysfunctions* are disorders in which one has difficulty functioning adequately while engaging in sexual behavior. *Paraphilias* refer to disorders in which sexual arousal occurs only in the context of inappropriate objects or individuals.

Test Yourself

Define the terms in questions 1–13.

1. Transsexualism

2. Hermaphrodites

3. Transvestites

4. Sex reassignment surgery

5. Sexual dysfunction

6. Sexual desire disorders

7. Sexual arousal disorders

8. Orgasm disorders

9. Sexual pain disorders

10. Fetishism

11. Transvestic fetishism

12. Paraphilias

13. Pedophilia

Questions 14–30 are true-false.

14. Hermaphrodites may require hormone treatments or surgery to correct anatomical abnormalities.

15. When there is a discrepancy between your personal belief and your biological sex, it is referred to as a gender identity disorder.

16. People with gender identity disorder are homosexuals.

17. Gender identity disorder is common.

18. A person's psychological sense of maleness or femaleness develops early, between 1½ and 3 years of age.

19. The most common treatment for transvestism is sex reassignment surgery.

20. Sexual dysfunctions can occur only in homosexual relationships.

21. Sexual dysfunctions can be situational, occurring only at certain times or with certain partners.

22. People with low sexual desire rarely fantasize about sex, infrequently masturbate and have sex once a month or less.

23. Inhibited orgasm is a disorder that is commonly seen in women seeking sexual treatment but rarely in men.

24. Dyspareunia is rare in men.

25. Sexual sadism is a paraphilia in which sexual arousal is associated with experiencing pain or humiliation.

26. Sexual ignorance can lead to sexual dysfunctions.

27. Voyeurism is a paraphilia.

28. The element of risk is unimportant to exhibitionists.

29. Victims of pedophilia tend to be young children while victims of incest tend to be daughters who are becoming sexually mature.

30. Some paraphiliacs also have extremely strong sex drives and engage in sexual activity frequently.

31. What is gender identity disorder?

32. Isn't gender identity disorder the same as hermaphrodism?

33. What are transvestites?

34. Are people with gender identity disorder gay?

35. How common is gender identity disorder?

36. What causes gender identity disorder?

37. How is gender identity disorder treated?

38. Can anyone have sex reassignment surgery?

39. What happens in sex reassignment surgery?

40. What are sexual dysfunctions?

41. Describe sexual desire disorders.

42. What are sexual arousal disorders?

43. What are orgasm disorders?

44. What is premature ejaculation?

45. Describe sexual pain disorders.

46. What causes sexual dysfunctions?

47. How are sexual dysfunctions treated?

48. What are paraphilias?

49. Describe fetishism.

50. What is transvestic fetishism?

51. What is the difference between voyeurism and exhibitionism?

52. What is the difference between sexual sadism and masochism?

53. Describe pedophilia.

54. What causes paraphilias?

55. How are paraphilias treated?

Check Yourself

1. Transsexualism is the former name for gender identity disorder, which reflects a discrepancy between one's personal belief and one's biological sex. (**Gender identity disorder**)

2. Hermaphrodites are born with ambiguous genitals and have hormonal or physical abnormalities. (**Gender identity disorder**)

3. Transvestites dress in the clothing of the opposite sex in order to become sexually aroused. (**Gender identity disorder**)

4. The most common treatment for gender identity disorder is sex reassignment surgery, which surgically alters anatomy to be consistent with the psychological sense of gender identity. (**Gender identity disorder**)

5. A sexual dysfunction is impaired functioning in any stage of the sexual response cycle. Sexual dysfunctions can occur in both heterosexual and homosexual relationships. (**Sexual dysfunctions**)

6. Sexual desire disorders are disorders associated with the first phase of the sexual response cycle characterized by a lacking of desire for sexual activity. (**Sexual dysfunctions**)

7. Sexual arousal disorders affect the second stage of the sexual response cycle, arousal. Individuals with this disorder have trouble becoming aroused, either having difficulty maintaining an erection or having enough vaginal lubrication. (**Sexual dysfunctions**)

8. Orgasm disorders occur in the last stage of the sexual response cycle. This disorder refers to the inability to achieve orgasm despite sufficient desire and arousal. (**Sexual dysfunctions**)

9. In sexual pain disorders, pain is associated with sexual activity. (**Sexual dysfunctions**)

10. Fetishism refers to a chronic, recurrent sexual attraction to objects. (**Paraphilias**)

11. In transvestic fetishism, men are sexually aroused by wearing women's clothing. (**Paraphilias**)

12. Paraphilias are sexual disorders in which sexual arousal occurs with regard to inappropriate objects. (**Paraphilias**)

13. Pedophilia is a paraphilia in which an adult has a strong sexual attraction toward children. (**Paraphilias**)

14. **True.** Hermaphrodites may require hormone treatments or surgery to correct anatomical abnormalities. (**Gender identity disorder**)

15. **True.** When there is a discrepancy between your personal belief and your biological sex, it is referred to as a gender identity disorder. (**Gender identity disorder**)

16. **False.** People with gender identity disorder are *not homosexuals*. (**Gender identity disorder**)

17. **False.** Gender identity disorder is *rare*. (**Gender identity disorder**)

18. **True.** A person's psychological sense of maleness or femaleness develops early, between 1½ and 3 years of age. **(Gender identity disorder)**

19. **False.** The most common treatment for *gender identity disorder* is sex reassignment surgery. **(Gender identity disorder)**

20. **False.** Sexual dysfunctions can occur *in both heterosexual and homosexual* relationships. **(Sexual dysfunctions)**

21. **True.** Sexual dysfunctions can be situational, occurring only at certain times or with certain partners. **(Sexual dysfunctions)**

22. **True.** People with low sexual desire rarely fantasize about sex, infrequently masturbate and have sex once a month or less. **(Sexual dysfunctions)**

23. **True.** Inhibited orgasm is a disorder that is commonly seen in women seeking sexual treatment but rarely in men. **(Sexual dysfunctions)**

24. **True.** Dyspareunia is rare in men. **(Sexual dysfunctions)**

25. **False.** Sexual *masochism* is a paraphilia in which sexual arousal is associated with experiencing pain or humiliation. **(Paraphilias)**

26. **True.** Sexual ignorance can lead to sexual dysfunctions. **(Sexual dysfunctions)**

27. **True.** Voyeurism is a paraphilia. **(Paraphilias)**

28. **False.** The element of risk is *important* to exhibitionists. **(Paraphilias)**

29. **True.** Victims of pedophilia tend to be young children while victims of incest tend to be daughters who are becoming sexually mature. **(Paraphilias)**

30. **True.** Some paraphiliacs also have extremely strong sex drives and engage in sexual activity frequently. **(Paraphilias)**

31. One's personal sense of one's identity as male or female is called gender identity. When there is a discrepancy between one's personal belief and biological sex, it is referred to as a gender identity disorder. Some people may feel that they are in the wrong body. This disorder used to be called transsexualism. People with gender identity disorder want to live their lives as the gender they believe they are. A male may have a psychological sense of being female and so would want to live his life as a female (or vice versa). **(Gender identity disorder)**

32. No. Hermaphrodites are born with ambiguous genitals and have hormonal or physical abnormalities. These individuals may require hormone treatments or surgery to correct these anatomical abnormalities. A person with gender identity disorder has no physical or hormonal abnormality. This person just has a psychological sense of being one gender and physical features (including genitalia) of the opposite sex. **(Gender identity disorder)**

33. Transvestites dress in the clothing of the opposite sex in order to become sexually aroused. Transvestic fetishism is a paraphilia and is not the same as gender identity disorder. A person with gender identity

disorder may dress in the clothing of the opposite sex in order to fulfill his or her psychological sense of being that gender, not to achieve sexual arousal. (**Gender identity disorder**)

34. No. Sometimes gay males may behave in an effeminate manner or dress in drag. However, these gay males do not think they are women nor do they want to be women. A person with gender identity disorder wants to be and feels as if he or she is the opposite sex. (**Gender identity disorder**)

35. Gender identity disorder is rare. Studies in Europe and Australia estimate the prevalence rate at between 1 in 24,000 to 1 in 37,000 in biological males and from 1 in 100,000 to 1 in 150,000 for females. (**Gender identity disorder**)

36. There are no known biological links to the development of gender identity disorder yet. There is no established connection between prenatal hormonal influence and later gender identity. Although we know that a person's psychological sense of maleness or femaleness develops early between 1½ and 3 years of age, we are not sure what causes development of an gender identity disorder. (**Gender identity disorder**)

37. The most common treatment is sex reassignment surgery which surgically alters anatomy to be consistent with the psychological sense of gender identity. This surgery is only done at a few clinics that specialize in sex reassignment surgery. Other possible treatments are psychosocial in nature and attempt to change gender identity. This psychological treatment has only succeeded with a few adult clients. (**Gender identity disorder**)

38. Usually, people must live as a member of the opposite sex for about two years in order to be sure about their decision to have surgery. These persons must also be stable psychologically, socially and financially. Most transsexuals who have this surgery successfully adjust to their new life. (**Gender identity disorder**)

39. For male-to-female transsexuals, the genitals are removed and a vagina is made. Hormones are given to grow breasts and facial hair is removed. For female-to-male transsexuals, a penis is artificially constructed and breasts are surgically removed. (**Gender identity disorder**)

40. The three stages of the sexual response cycle are desire, arousal, and orgasm. A sexual dysfunction is impaired functioning in any one of these stages. Sexual dysfunctions can occur in both heterosexual and homosexual relationships. Also, pain can be associated with sexual behavior leading to more sexual dysfunctions. Sexual dysfunctions can be chronic or acquired. Chronic means they last a lifetime and acquired means that they arise at a particular time prior to which functioning was normal. Sexual dysfunctions might also be situational, occurring only at certain times or with certain partners. Generalized sexual dysfunctions occur every time a person has sex. (**Sexual dysfunctions**)

41. Sexual desire disroders are associated with the first phase of the sexual response cycle. Hypoactive sexual desire refers to a lack of interest in sexual activities. Almost half of all those attending sexuality clinics do so because of low desire and slightly more than half of these (55 percent) are males. People with low sexual desire rarely fantasize about sex, infrequently masturbate and have sex once a month or less. Sexual aversion disorder reflects an extreme and enduring dislike of sexual contact or activities. There is no interest in having sex and sexual touch may evoke negative emotions. In some cases, the main difficulty might actually be a panic disorder that has become associated with sexual acts. In other cases, sexual acts may trigger traumatic memories that are less severe than those associated with post-traumatic stress disorder. (**Sexual dysfunctions**)

42. Sexual arousal disorders affect the second stage of the sexual response cycle, arousal. Individuals with sexual arousal disorders have trouble becoming aroused, either having difficulty maintaining an erection or having enough vaginal lubrication. There is no problem with sexual desire here. Male erectile disorder

refers to a reoccurring inability in men to achieve or maintain adequate erection and used to be called impotence. *Female sexual arousal disorder* refers to a recurrent inability to achieve or maintain sufficient vaginal lubrication and swelling until completion of sexual activity and used to be called frigidity. Women may be able to compensate by using lubricants. Male erectile disorder is common, with estimates of prevalence ranging from 4 percent to 10 percent of adult males. Female sexual arousal disorder has been estimated to occur in 11 percent to 48 percent of adult women. These estimates are not exact because of lack of acknowledgment of a problem among women, an inexact relationship between adequate sexual functioning and sexual satisfaction and the fact that these categories of disorders are not mutually exclusive. (**Sexual dysfunctions**)

43. Orgasm disorders occur in the last stage of the sexual response cycle. Inhibited orgasm is a disorder that is commonly seen in women seeking sexual treatment but rarely in men. This disorder refers to the inability to achieve orgasm despite sufficient desire and arousal. *Female orgasmic disorder* is a recurrent delay or absence of orgasm following normal excitement and is also called inhibited female orgasm. *Male orgasmic disorder* is a recurrent delay or absence of orgasm following normal excitement and is also called inhibited male orgasm. Prevalence studies estimate that about 5 percent to 10 percent of women experience female orgasmic disorder. (**Sexual dysfunctions**)

44. Premature ejaculation is a disorder in which there is recurring ejaculation occurring before a man wants it to, with minimal sexual stimulation. The frequency of premature ejaculation is high with a prevalence rate around 37 percent reported in community samples. (**Sexual dysfunctions**)

45. In sexual pain disorders, pain is associated with sexual activity. There are two types of sexual pain disorders: dyspareunia and vaginismus. *Dyspareunia* refers to recurring pain in either sex occurring at any time during sexual activity (before, after or during sexual intercourse). Dyspareunia is only diagnosed if all possible medical reasons are ruled out. Dyspareunia is rare in men, with prevalence estimates of about 1 percent to 5 percent in men. It is more common in females with estimates ranging from 8 percent to 33 percent in community samples. Vaginismus is more common than dyspareunia. *Vaginismus* occurs in women and refers to recurring involuntary spasms of pelvic muscles that interfere with intercourse. (**Sexual dysfunctions**)

46. Most sexual dysfunctions are not caused solely by biological or psychological factors but by an interaction of these factors. Some biological causes that may affect sexual functioning are neurological diseases, vascular disease, chronic illness and prescription medications. Alcohol and other drugs also interfere with normal sexual functioning. Psychological factors that may influence sexual functioning are anxiety and distraction. Performance anxiety which has cognitive and arousal components may affect sexual functioning. When in a sexual situation, dysfunctional people may react with negative emotions. This individual may be focused on negative thoughts which interfere with his or her ability to become sexually aroused. There are also social factors that may contribute to sexual dysfunction such as negative attitudes, negative sexual experiences, deterioration in interpersonal relationships and poor sexual skills. (**Sexual dysfunctions**)

47. There are both medical and psychosocial treatments for sexual dysfunctions. Education is an important treatment for sexual dysfunction. Sexual ignorance can lead to sexual dysfunctions. Masters and Johnson made many advances in sex therapy, outlining treatments for many sexual dysfunctions. Their approach uses intense psychotherapy and basic sexual education, modifies sexual myths, and tries to eliminate performance anxiety. (**Sexual dysfunctions**)

48. Paraphilias are sexual disorders in which sexual arousal occurs with regard to inappropriate objects. There are several paraphilias: fetishism, transvestic fetishism, voyeurism, exhibitionism, sexual sadism, sexual masochism, and pedophilia. (**Paraphilias**)

49. Fetishism refers to a chronic, recurrent sexual attraction to objects. The individual may have sexual urges toward and sexual fantasies and behaviors involving unusual objects. This behavior causes significant distress or functional impairment. Fetishism can be associated with inanimate objects or specific sources of tactile stimulation, such as clothing made out of specific materials, perhaps leather, rubber, etc. People with fetishes may also be attracted to a specific part of the body. **(Paraphilias)**

50. In transvestic fetishism, men are sexually aroused by wearing women's clothing. This is also called cross-dressing. Many of these men may be married and their wives may accept their behavior if it is kept private. **(Paraphilias)**

51. Voyeurism involves observing people undressing or naked. The people being observed do not know they are being watched by the voyeur. In contrast, exhibitionism refers to achieving sexual arousal and gratification from exposing one's genitals to strangers. The element of risk is important to exhibitionists. Sometimes these two disorders may occur in the same individual. **(Paraphilias)**

52. Sexual sadism is a paraphilia in which sexual arousal is associated with the infliction of pain or humiliation upon others. Sexual masochism is a paraphilia in which sexual arousal is associated with experiencing pain or humiliation. **(Paraphilias)**

53. Pedophilia is a paraphilia in which an adult has a strong sexual attraction toward children. If the children are members of the pedophile's family, the pedophilia is referred to as incest. Victims of pedophilia tend to be young children while victims of incest tend to be daughters who are becoming sexually mature (adolescent or preadolescent). Child molesters rationalize their behavior as teaching or loving the child but rarely acknowledge the psychological harm done to the child. **(Paraphilias)**

54. Case studies reveal that deviant patterns of sexual arousal develop in the context of other sexual and social problems. Many times, the inability to have adequate sexual relationships seems to be associated with developing inappropriate sexual objects. With others, early experiences may lead to paraphilias. Also important is the nature of a person's sexual fantasies. Early sexual fantasies that are reinforced through the pleasure associated with masturbation may contribute to the development of fetishes. Some paraphiliacs also have extremely strong sex drives and engage in sexual activity frequently. **(Paraphilias)**

55. There are several psychosocial treatments for paraphilias that seem to be promising but they are only offered at specialized treatment facilities. These treatments typically involve some behavioral therapy aimed at changing pleasurable associations to a neutral one. Also, relapse prevention is used to detect signs of temptation and replace sexual urges with self-control measures. There are also some drug treatments that eliminate sexual desire and fantasy as long as the drug is taken. This may be useful for the most dangerous sex offenders. The psychosocial treatments have success rates ranging from 70 percent to 100 percent over 10 years; however, this is based on a small sample. **(Paraphilias)**

Grade Yourself

Circle the numbers of the questions you missed, then fill in the total incorrect for each topic. If you answered more than three questions incorrectly, you need to focus on that topic. (If a topic has fewer than three questions and you had at least one wrong, we suggest you study that topic also. Read your textbook or a review book, or ask your teacher for help.)

Subject: Sexual Disorders

Topic	Question Numbers	Number Incorrect
Gender identity disorder	1, 2, 3, 4, 14, 15, 16, 17, 18, 19, 31, 32, 33, 34, 35, 36, 37, 38, 39	
Sexual dysfunctions	5, 6, 7, 8, 9, 20, 21, 22, 23, 24, 26, 40, 41, 42, 43, 44, 45, 46, 47	
Paraphilias	10, 11, 12, 13, 25, 27, 28, 29, 30, 48, 49, 50, 51, 52, 53, 54, 55	

Schizophrenia

16

Brief Yourself

Schizophrenia is a broad category of cognitive and affective dysfunctions that include delusions, hallucinations, disorganized speech and behavior, and inappropriate affect.

Schizophrenic symptoms are categorized as either positive, active manifestations of abnormal behavior, or negative deficits in normal behaviors. There are five types of schizophrenia: *paranoid, disorganized, catatonic, undifferentiated,* and *residual*. Schizophrenia is typically chronic with onset in early adulthood. There are many factors linked to the etiology of schizophrenia including genetic factors, brain damage and psychosocial stressors. Relapse appears to be associated with hostile family environments. Treatment for schizophrenia typically involves medications such as neuroleptics. There are also other psychotic disorders: schizophreniform, schizoaffective, delusional, brief psychotic and shared psychotic disorders.

Test Yourself

Define the terms in questions 1–7.

1. Positive symptoms

2. Negative symptoms

3. Delusions

4. Hallucinations

5. Waxy flexibility

6. Alogia

7. Avolition

Questions 8–27 are true-false.

8. The term *schizophrenia* was introduced by Freud in 1908 and meant "split mind."

9. Schizophrenia may affect 10 out of every 100 people at some point.

10. Schizophrenia refers to a split personality or many personalities.

11. Those schizophrenics who exhibit positive symptoms respond well to medication and have a good prognosis.

12. Common among schizophrenics are delusions of persecution, thoughts that people are out to get them.

13. The most common type of hallucinations among schizophrenics are visual hallucinations.

14. An example of disorganized behavior is inappropriate affect, which is an inappropriate emotional response.

15. About 66 percent of schizophrenics exhibit flat affect.

16. The paranoid subtype of schizophrenia is characterized by primary symptoms of delusions and hallucinations which are marked by persistent themes of persecution by others or grandiosity.

17. The disorganized subtype has a stronger genetic component and better prognosis than other subtypes.

18. In the disorganized subtype, motor disturbances are the primary symptoms.

19. The residual subtype is used to categorize those who have had at least one episode of schizophrenia but no longer display the major symptoms.

20. Complications during pregnancy have not been implicated as a causal factor in schizophrenia.

21. Evidence gathered from twin and adoptions studies demonstrate a weak genetic component.

22. There is about a 33 percent chance that you will develop schizophrenia if your parent has schizophrenia.

23. Prior to the 1950's people with schizophrenia were sometimes treated with prefrontal lobotomies.

24. Neuroleptics help relieve thought difficulties and reduce negative symptoms.

25. Delusional disorder is a psychotic disorder that is characterized by a persistent delusion but no other symptoms of schizophrenia.

26. Schizoaffective disorder is a psychotic disorder that includes symptoms of schizophrenia and a personality disorder.

27. Delusional disorder is rare and onset is late, typically in the 40's.

28. Describe schizophrenia.

29. What is the difference between positive and negative schizophrenic symptoms?

30. What are delusions?

31. Describe hallucinations.

32. What is meant by "disorganized speech"?

33. What is meant by "disorganized behavior"?

34. What is "flat affect"?

35. Discuss three other negative symptoms.

36. Describe the five subtypes of schizophrenia.

37. What causes schizophrenia?

38. What do we know about genetic influences in schizophrenia?

39. Is schizophrenia treated medically or psychologically?

40. What are the other psychotic disorders?

Check Yourself

1. Positive symptoms refer to distorted behaviors such as delusions, hallucinations and disorganized speech. **(Schizophrenia description and symptoms)**

2. Negative symptoms indicate deficiencies in normal behavior such as flat affect, speech deficits and motivational deficits. **(Schizophrenia description and symptoms)**

3. Delusions are psychotic symptoms of strong irrational beliefs. People may have delusions of grandeur, believing that they are famous or important people, such as Jesus Christ, Napoleon, etc. **(Schizophrenia description and symptoms)**

4. Hallucinations are psychotic symptoms consisting of perceptual disturbances in which things are seen, heard or sensed in the absence of any actual stimuli. **(Schizophrenia description and symptoms)**

5. Waxy flexibility refers to a person's idea that others can position his or her body into strange positions which are then held for long periods of time. **(Schizophrenia description and symptoms)**

6. Alogia is a deficiency in the amount or content of speech. **(Schizophrenia description and symptoms)**

7. Avolition refers to apathy or an inability to begin and maintain important activities. **(Schizophrenia description and symptoms)**

8. **False.** The term *schizophrenia* was introduced by *Bleuler* in 1908 and meant "split mind." **(Schizophrenia description and symptoms)**

9. **False.** Schizophrenia may affect *1* out of every 100 people at some point. **(Schizophrenia description and symptoms)**

10. **False.** Schizophrenia *does not refer* to a split personality or many personalities. Schizophrenia is a psychotic disorder that involves disturbances in thinking, emotions, speech and behavior. **(Schizophrenia description and symptoms)**

11. **True.** Those schizophrenics who exhibit positive symptoms respond well to medication and have a good prognosis. **(Schizophrenia description and symptoms)**

12. **True.** Common among schizophrenics are delusions of persecution, thoughts that people are out to get them. **(Schizophrenia description and symptoms)**

13. **False.** The most common type of hallucinations among schizophrenics are *auditory* hallucinations. **(Schizophrenia description and symptoms)**

14. **False.** An example of disorganized behavior is not inappropriate affect, which is an inappropriate emotional response. **(Schizophrenia description and symptoms)**

15. **True.** About 66 percent of schizophrenics exhibit flat affect. **(Schizophrenia description and symptoms)**

16. **True.** The paranoid subtype of schizophrenia is characterized by primary symptoms of delusions and hallucinations which are marked by persistent themes of persecution by others or grandiosity. (**Types of schizophrenia**)

17. **False.** The *paranoid* subtype has a stronger genetic component and better prognosis than other subtypes. (**Types of schizophrenia**)

18. **False.** In the *catatonic* subtype, motor disturbances are the primary symptoms. (**Types of schizophrenia**)

19. **True.** The residual subtype is used to categorize those who have had at least one episode of schizophrenia but no longer display the major symptoms. (**Types of schizophrenia**)

20. **False.** Complications during pregnancy *have been* implicated as a causal factor in schizophrenia. (**Etiology of schizophrenia**)

21. **False.** Evidence gathered from twin and adoptions studies demonstrate a *strong* genetic component. (**Etiology of schizophrenia**)

22. **False.** There is about a *13 percent* chance that you will develop schizophrenia if your parent has schizophrenia. (**Etiology of schizophrenia**)

23. **True.** Prior to the 1950's people with schizophrenia were sometimes treated with prefrontal lobotomies. (**Treatment of schizophrenia**)

24. **False.** Neuroleptics help relieve thought difficulties and reduce *positive* symptoms. (**Treatment of schizophrenia**)

25. **True.** Delusional disorder is a psychotic disorder that is characterized by a persistent delusion but no other symptoms of schizophrenia. (**Other psychotic disorders**)

26. **False.** Schizoaffective disorder is a psychotic disorder that includes symptoms of schizophrenia and *major mood disorder*. (**Other psychotic disorders**)

27. **True.** Delusional disorder is rare and onset is late, typically in the 40's. (**Other psychotic disorders**)

28. Schizophrenia is a psychotic disorder that involves disturbances in thinking, emotions, speech and behavior. Schizophrenia disturbs perception and all aspects of functioning. Treatment is possible yet complete recovery is rare. Schizophrenia may affect 1 out of every 100 people at some point. *Schizophrenia* was a term introduced by Bleuler in 1908 and meant "split mind." He believed that underlying the unusual symptoms of schizophrenia was a separation of the basic personality functions such as emotion, thought and perception. This has lead to the common misconception that schizophrenia refers to a split personality or many personalities, which is not the case. For a person to be diagnosed with schizophrenia, he or she must display two or more of the following symptoms for a significant amount of time during one month: delusions, hallucinations, disorganized speech, disorganized behavior and negative symptoms. (**Schizophrenia description and symptoms**)

29. Positive symptoms refer to distorted behaviors such as delusions, hallucinations and disorganized speech. Negative symptoms indicate deficiencies in normal behavior such as flat affect, speech deficits and motivational deficits. Those schizophrenics who exhibit positive symptoms respond well to medication and have a good prognosis. Individuals with negative symptoms respond poorly to

medication, have intellectual impairments and a poor prognosis. (**Schizophrenia description and symptoms**)

30. Delusions are psychotic symptoms of strong irrational beliefs. People may have delusions of grandeur, believing that they are famous or important people, such as Jesus Christ, Napoleon, etc. Common among schizophrenics are delusions of persecution, thoughts that people are out to get them. (**Schizophrenia description and symptoms**)

31. Hallucinations are psychotic symptoms consisting of perceptual disturbances in which things are seen, heard or sensed in the absence of any actual stimuli. The most common type of hallucinations among schizophrenics are auditory hallucinations, hearing voices. (**Schizophrenia description and symptoms**)

32. Disorganized speech is another symptom of schizophrenia. It involves a style of speaking that is incoherent and lacks logical patterns. People with schizophrenia sometimes jump from topic to topic when speaking. They may also never directly answer questions but go off on some tangent that is seemingly unrelated. They also move conversation topics to unrelated areas, referred to as loose associations. (**Schizophrenia description and symptoms**)

33. Schizophrenics engage in active behaviors that are considered to be positive symptoms. One of these is *catatonia* which is a disorder of movement involving immobility or agitated movements. Examples of agitated movements include pacing and the waving of arms. Immobility means that the person is fixed in one position for a long period of time. Also characteristic of some schizophrenics is waxy flexibility, which refers to the idea that others can position the body of this person into strange positions which are then maintained or held for long periods of time, like moving parts of a doll into any position you desire. One example of affective dysfunction is inappropriate affect, which is an inappropriate emotional response, such as laughing at a funeral. (**Schizophrenia description and symptoms**)

34. Flat affect refers to being emotionless. There may be toneless speech and vacant gaze when you would expect some kind of emotion. About 66 percent of schizophrenics exhibit flat affect. However, because they appear emotionless on the outside, one cannot assume that they are not experiencing emotions. It could be that they do not exhibit emotions but keep them inside. (**Schizophrenia description and symptoms**)

35. Another negative symptom is called *avolition*, which refers to apathy or an inability to begin and maintain important activities. People exhibiting this symptom show little interest in any activity; even the most basic hygienic activities are seemingly unimportant. *Alogia* is a deficiency in the amount or content of speech. People with alogia may respond to questions with brevity and appear uninterested in the conversation. Sometimes alogia involves slow or delayed responses. *Anhedonia* refers to the inability of a schizophrenic to experience pleasure. Schizophrenics often say they no longer enjoy previously pleasurable activities. (**Schizophrenia description and symptoms**)

36. The paranoid subtype of schizophrenia, the first subtype, is characterized by primary symptoms of delusions and hallucinations. Speech, motor behavior and emotions are intact. The delusions and hallucinations are marked by persistent themes of persecution by others or grandiosity. This subtype appears to have a stronger genetic component and better prognosis than other subtypes. The *disorganized subtype* features disrupted speech and behavior, flat or silly affect, and disjointed delusions and hallucinations. This subtype was previously called hebephrenic. The delusions and hallucinations are not organized around a theme. People with this subtype often display symptoms early and often have chronic problems. In the *catatonic subtype*, motor disturbances are the primary symptoms. There may be rigidity, agitation and odd mannerisms. These individuals may also repeat or mimic the words or movements of others, called echolalia and echopraxia, respectively. This subtype of schizophrenia is rare. The *undifferentiated subtype* is used to categorize those individuals who meet the diagnostic criteria for schizophrenia but not for one of its

subtypes. The *residual subtype* is used to categorize those who have had at least one episode of schizophrenia but no longer display the major symptoms. These individuals may have beliefs that are not severe enough to be called delusional, social withdrawal, strange thoughts, inactivity and flat affect. (**Types of schizophrenia**)

37. Schizophrenia is a complicated disorder which may have multifactorial etiology, many causal factors. Some studies implicate genetic influences, neurotransmitters such as dopamine, brain structure, viral infection, complications of pregnancy, unstable early family environment, and stress. All of these factors may play a role; some may play a role in some cases but not all. You can see that there is no simple nor definitive answer. (**Etiology of schizophrenia**)

38. We know that genes may make some people vulnerable to developing schizophrenia. Evidence gathered from twin and adoptions studies demonstrate a strong genetic component. You can have genes that predispose you to have schizophrenia, not develop schizophrenia yourself and your children will inherit these genes from you. There is about a 13 percent chance that you will develop schizophrenia if your parent has schizophrenia. (**Etiology of schizophrenia**)

39. Both. Prior to the 1950's people with schizophrenia were sometimes treated with prefrontal lobotomies, which severed the part of the brain connecting the frontal lobes to the lower part of the brain. Then a breakthrough came when several drugs were introduced that treated the schizophrenic symptoms, in the 1950's. These drugs, called neuroleptics, help relieve thought difficulties and reduce positive symptoms. However, they do not eliminate the negative symptoms. Some drugs help some people. The process of finding the right drug for a patient is by trial and error. A newer drug, clozapine, is now available and appears to help those who did not respond to other medications. There are also psychological treatments. These psychosocial treatments involve teaching social and independent living skills and working with family members to help them better understand schizophrenia. Traditional insight therapy does not work with schizophrenics due to their thought and speech difficulties. The most promising treatments combine medication and education, such as skills training and family education. (**Treatment of schizophrenia**)

40. *Schizophreniform disorder* is a psychotic disorder featuring the symptoms of schizophrenia but lasting less than six months. These symptoms come and go quickly and the person resumes a normal life. *Schizoaffective disorder* is a psychotic disorder that includes symptoms of schizophrenia and major mood disorder. This disorder is chronic and has a poor prognosis. *Delusional disorder* is a psychotic disorder that is characterized by a persistent delusion but no other symptoms of schizophrenia. Delusions are beliefs that are contrary to reality. These delusions last for many years and may result in some social isolation. These delusions are not as bizarre as the ones experienced by schizophrenics. Delusional disorder is rare and onset is late, typically in the 40's. *Brief psychotic disorder* involves delusions, hallucinations, or disorganized speech or behavior that lasts less than one month. This disorder often occurs as a reaction to severe stress. These individuals return to their previous level of functioning. *Shared psychotic disorder* refers to a person developing a delusion that is similar to that of a person he or she shares a close relationship with. (**Other psychotic disorders**)

Grade Yourself

Circle the numbers of the questions you missed, then fill in the total incorrect for each topic. If you answered more than three questions incorrectly, you need to focus on that topic. (If a topic has fewer than three questions and you had at least one wrong, we suggest you study that topic also. Read your textbook or a review book, or ask your teacher for help.)

Subject: Schizophrenia

Topic	Question Numbers	Number Incorrect
Schizophrenia description and symptoms	1, 2, 3, 4, 5, 6, 7, 8, 9, 10, 11, 12, 13, 14, 15, 28, 29, 30, 31, 32, 33, 34, 35	
Types of schizophrenia	16, 17, 18, 19, 36	
Etiology of schizophrenia	20, 21, 22, 37, 38	
Treatment of schizophrenia	23, 24, 39	
Other psychotic disorders	25, 26, 27, 40	

Cognitive Disorders

17

Brief Yourself

Typically, cognitive disorder develop later in life, as one grows older. Cognitive disorders first become apparent when a person is in his or her fifties. As our population grows older, these disorders will become increasingly prevalent. These disorders involve a deficit in cognition or memory. There are three categories of cognitive disorders: *delirium*, *dementia* and *amnestic disorders*. Delirium is often transitory and is manifested by confusion and disorientation. Dementia, however, is gradual and progressive, resulting in deteriorating cognitive abilities. Amnestic disorder referred to a memory dysfunction brought on by a disease, toxicity, or drug use.

Test Yourself

Define the terms in questions 1–6.

1. Delirium

2. Dementia

3. Agnosia

4. Facial agnosia

5. Vascular dementia

6. Korsakoff syndrome

Questions 7–13 are true-false.

7. People with delirium cannot think or reason clearly.

8. Delirium is less common among older adults and people with cancer or AIDS.

9. Full recovery of those with delirium is not expected in most cases.

10. Delirium caused by drug withdrawal is usually treated by benzodiazepines.

11. Dementia can be a consequence of medical conditions or drug abuse.

12. Dementia of the Alzheimer's type is the most common type of dementia.

13. Amnestic disorders involve a deterioration in the ability to transfer information from short-term to long-term memory.

14. What is delirium?

15. What is the prognosis for delirium?

16. What causes delirium?

17. How is delirium treated?

18. Describe dementia.

19. What is Alzheimer's type dementia?

20. How many people have Alzheimer's dementia?

21. What is vascular dementia?

22. What causes dementia?

23. How is dementia treated?

24. Describe amnestic disorders.

 # Check Yourself

1. Delirium involves a loss of clarity in cognitive processes such as confusion and disorientation. **(Delirium)**

2. Dementia is a deterioration of cognitive functioning which includes memory loss, recognition problems, planning problems and problems with abstract reasoning. **(Dementia)**

3. Agnosia is the inability to recognize or name objects experienced by those with dementia. **(Dementia)**

4. Facial agnosia is the inability to recognize familiar faces. **(Dementia)**

5. Vascular dementia is a progressive brain disorder caused by blocked blood flow to the brain. **(Dementia)**

6. Korsakoff syndrome is an amnestic disorder caused by damage to the brain's relay stations that is due to vascular damage or alcohol abuse. **(Amnestic disorders)**

7. **True.** People with delirium cannot think or reason clearly. **(Delirium)**

8. **False.** Delirium is *more* common among older adults and people with cancer or AIDS. **(Delirium)**

9. **False.** Full recovery of those with delirium *is expected* in most cases within a few weeks. **(Delirium)**

10. **True.** Delirium caused by drug withdrawal is usually treated by benzodiazepines. **(Delirium)**

11. **True.** Dementia can be a consequence of medical conditions or drug abuse. **(Dementia)**

12. **True.** Dementia of the Alzheimer's type is the most common type of dementia. **(Dementia)**

13. **True.** Amnestic disorders involve a deterioration in the ability to transfer information from short-term to long-term memory. **(Amnestic disorders)**

14. Delirium usually hits a person rapidly and may be a temporary condition. It involves a loss of clarity in cognitive processes such as confusion and disorientation. There may also be deficits in memory and language. People with delirium cannot think or reason clearly. **(Delirium)**

15. People with delirium often improve quickly, sometimes within days. Full recovery is expected in most cases within a few weeks. **(Delirium)**

16. Delirium may be a sign of a medical condition that is causing brain dysfunction. There are many medical conditions that can cause delirium including drug and poison intoxication, drug withdrawal, head injury, infections and other brain traumas. **(Delirium)**

17. Delirium is treated by first examining any medical conditions that may have resulted in delirium. Delirium caused by drug withdrawal is usually treated by benzodiazepines which have a calming effect. Psychosocial treatments may also be used to help the person deal with accompanying problems like anxiety and hallucinations. Letting the patient be involved in all treatment aspects helps him or her maintain a sense of control. **(Delirium)**

18. Dementia occurs gradually and refers to a deterioration of cognitive functioning. There may be memory loss, recognition problems, planning problems and problems with abstract reasoning. The person may also experience a sense of frustration and discouragement. Dementia can be a consequence of medical conditions or drug abuse. The dementia associated with Alzheimer's disease is irreversible. Some other dementias, brought on by infection, can be treated. People with dementia may not be able to recognize or name objects (agnosia) or may not be able to recognize familiar faces (facial agnosia). There are also emotional changes associated with dementia such as depression, aggression and apathy. **(Dementia)**

19. Dementia of the Alzheimer's type, the gradual onset of cognitive deficits caused by having Alzheimer's disease, is the most common type of dementia. People with this type of dementia cannot recall new or previously learned material. The main symptom is memory impairment. **(Dementia)**

20. About four million Americans are believed to suffer from this type of dementia. The average survival time for Alzheimer's disorder is about eight years. Onset can occur in the 40's or 50's but typically occurs in either the 60's or 70's. **(Dementia)**

21. Vascular dementia is a progressive brain disorder caused by blocked blood flow to the brain. Vascular dementia is second only to Alzheimer's as a cause of dementia. The cognitive deficits differ in each person but often resemble those found in Alzheimer's dementia. The lifetime risk of having this dementia is about 4 percent. **(Dementia)**

22. Certain diseases like Alzheimer's and Huntington's disease make some individuals vulnerable to dementia. Also, brain injury or drug use can cause cognitive declines. **(Dementia)**

23. There are some medications that can enhance the cognitive abilities of those with Alzheimer's in the short-term. However, there are questions about their long-term effectiveness. Psychosocial treatments do not try to enhance cognitive abilities but rather focus on improving the quality of life for patients and their families. People can be taught skills to help them compensate for cognitive losses. **(Dementia)**

24. Amnestic disorders are characterized by a deterioration in the ability to transfer information from short-term to long-term memory due to head trauma or drug use. There is no loss of other higher level cognitive functions as in dementia. Korsakoff syndrome is an amnestic disorder caused by damage to the brain's relay stations (thalamus) that is due to vascular damage or alcohol abuse. **(Amnestic disorders)**

Grade Yourself

Circle the numbers of the questions you missed, then fill in the total incorrect for each topic. If you answered more than three questions incorrectly, you need to focus on that topic. (If a topic has fewer than three questions and you had at least one wrong, we suggest you study that topic also. Read your textbook or a review book, or ask your teacher for help.)

Subject: Cognitive Disorders

Topic	Question Numbers	Number Incorrect
Delirium	1, 7, 8, 9, 10, 14, 15, 16, 17	
Dementia	2, 3, 4, 5, 11, 12, 18, 19, 20, 21, 22, 23	
Amnestic disorders	6, 13, 24	

Clinical Assessment

18

Brief Yourself

Clinical assessment is a systematic evaluation of a person's psychological, biological and social characteristics when presenting for treatment for a psychological disorder. The clinician should at first collect information from a variety of sources. Then the clinician narrows the focus to areas that are problematic. Three concepts are important in determining the value of an assessment: *reliability*, *validity* and *standardization*. Reliability refers to the consistency of a measure over time. Validity refers to the degree to which a measurement technique measures what it claims to measure. Standardization refers to application of norms and consistent procedures across different measurements. Clinical assessment includes several techniques including interviews, physical examination, behavioral observation and psychological tests.

Test Yourself

Define the terms in questions 1–10.

1. Reliability

2. Validity

3. Standardization

4. Clinical interview

5. Mental status exam

6. Sensorium

7. Projective tests

8. MMPI

9. Rorschach inkblot test

10. Neuropsychological tests

Questions 11–19 are true-false.

11. Validity refers to the consistency of a measure over time.

12. Reliability ensures that similar procedures are used in measurement across different situations.

13. Clinicians want to gather information about a person's family, sexual history, religious views, education and cultural concerns.

14. Affect reflects the predominant feeling of the person.

15. Mood reflects the feelings that accompany thoughts and words.

16. Rate, continuity, and content of speech help a clinician assess cognitive functioning.

17. Observations focus on the antecedents of a behavior, the behavior itself, and the consequences of that behavior.

18. Objective tests have one advantage over projective tests: they are harder to fake.

19. There is some overlap between intelligence tests and neuropsychological tests.

20. Describe the three concepts needed to understand assessment.

21. What is a clinical interview?

22. Describe the mental status exam.

23. What is meant by behavioral assessment?

24. What does the clinician try to observe?

25. What are psychological tests?

26. Describe projective tests.

27. Are objective tests more reliable?

28. Do clinicians use intelligence tests also?

29. What are neuropsychological tests?

 Check Yourself

1. Reliability refers to the consistency of a measure over time. (**Assessment concepts**)

2. Validity refers to the fact that an instrument or test measures what it claims to measure. (**Assessment concepts**)

3. Standardization ensures that similar procedures are used in measurement across different situations. (**Assessment concepts**)

4. The clinical interview is used by most mental health professionals to gather information on current and past behaviors and feelings. (**Clinical interviews**)

5. The mental status exam is usually given during a clinical interview and is an evaluation of the client's judgment, temporal orientation, and emotional state. This exam covers five categories: physical appearance, thought processes, emotions, intellectual functioning and sensorium. (**Clinical interviews**)

6. Sensorium refers to a general awareness of one's environment. (**Clinical interviews**)

7. Projective tests present a person with ambiguous stimuli to respond to. It is believed that a person's response reflects underlying psychological processes and will reveal unconscious conflicts. (**Psychological tests**)

8. The most widely used personality inventory in the United States is the Minnesota Multiphasic Personality Inventory (MMPI). (**Psychological tests**)

9. The most widely used projective test contains a series of 10 cards with inkblots on them, the Rorschach inkblot test. (**Psychological tests**)

10. Neuropsychological tests assess brain and nervous system functioning by testing performance on certain tasks. (**Neuropsychological tests**)

11. **False.** *Reliability* refers to the consistency of a measure over time. (**Assessment concepts**)

12. **False.** *Standardization* ensures that similar procedures are used in measurement across different situations. (**Assessment concepts**)

13. **True.** Clinicians want to gather information about a person's family, sexual history, religious views, education and cultural concerns. (**Clinical interviews**)

14. **False.** *Mood* reflects the predominant feeling of the person. (**Clinical interviews**)

15. **False.** *Affect* reflects the feelings that accompany thoughts and words. (**Clinical interviews**)

16. **True.** Rate, continuity, and content of speech help a clinician assess cognitive functioning. (**Clinical interviews**)

17. **True.** Observations focus on the antecedents of a behavior, the behavior itself, and the consequences of that behavior. (**Behavioral observations**)

18. **False.** *Projective tests* have one advantage over objective tests: they are harder to fake. (**Psychological tests**)

19. **True.** There is some overlap between intelligence tests and neuropsychological tests. (**Neuropsychological tests**)

20. The first is reliability which refers to the consistency of a measure over time. Consistency in diagnosis is important. You would expect someone who went to several clinicians presenting the same symptoms to get the same diagnosis. The degree to which this is true is called reliability. Validity is important also. Measures should measure what they say they measure, otherwise we have no idea what we are measuring. Standardization ensures that similar procedures are used in measurement across different situations. There should be standard procedures for administering, scoring and interpreting a test or measure. Also, these measures are often given to large groups to get a reference point or standard against which to compare a person's performance. (**Assessment concepts**)

21. The clinical interview is used by most mental health professionals to gather information on current and past behaviors and feelings. Also, it is useful to gather information about a person's life history. Clinicians focus on the present problem and try to get more information about it. Clinicians also want to get information about a person's family, sexual history, religious views, education and cultural concerns. One of the first things done in a clinical interview is the mental status exam. (**Clinical interviews**)

22. This is usually given during a clinical interview and is an evaluation of the client's judgment, temporal orientation, and emotional state. This exam covers five categories: physical appearance, thought processes, emotions, intellectual functioning and sensorium. Physical appearance means that the clinician notices the person's dress, posture, facial expressions and overt behaviors. When talking to a client, the clinician can get a good idea of a person's thought processes. Rate, continuity, and content of speech help a clinician assess cognitive functioning. The clinician can also detect if any delusions or hallucinations are present. Determining mood or emotion is an important part of this exam. Mood reflects the predominant feeling of the person. Affect reflects the feelings that accompany thoughts and words. Clinicians also try to roughly estimate a person's intellectual functioning by talking to him or her. One can measure intellectual functioning by vocabulary, use of

metaphors and abstractions, and memory. Sensorium refers to a general awareness of one's environment. Sensorium can be measured by assessing the people's self, time and place orientation. Do they know who they are? Do they know where they are? Do they know what day and time it is? (**Clinical interviews**)

23. Behavioral assessment involves formally assessing a person's thoughts, feelings and behavior in specific contexts. This information is used to try to explain why the individual is having problems. Sometimes interviews are not as useful as they could be because the client is a young child, is withholding information, or has limited verbal skills. Behavioral assessment identifies target behaviors which are observed in order to determine what influences these behaviors. If actually going to a person's home, work or school is not feasible, an analogous situation may be set up to see how the person behaves. (**Behavioral observations**)

24. Observations focus on the antecedents of a behavior, the behavior itself, and the consequences of that behavior. Observation can be informal, observing and making mental notes, or more formal and structured, such as using rating scales to measure behaviors. (**Behavioral observations**)

25. Psychological tests are often used to assess psychological disorders and should have good reliability and validity. There are two types of psychological tests: projective and objective tests. (**Psychological tests**)

26. Projective tests require a person to respond to an ambiguous stimuli. It is believed that a person's response reflects underlying psychological processes and will reveal unconscious conflicts. People are thought to "project" their own personality and fears onto the test. The most widely used projective test contains a series of 10 cards with inkblots on them, the Rorschach inkblot test. The person is shown a card and asked to tell the clinician what he or she sees. Another widely used test, the Thematic Apperception Test (TAT) contains cards with pictures on them and the client is asked to make up a story to go along with the picture. Projective tests have one advantage over objective tests: they are harder to fake because there is no right or wrong answer. Projective tests are commonly used; however, they lack the reliability and validity of other instruments. They are useful in some situations but not as a sole diagnostic tool. (**Psychological tests**)

27. Yes, objective tests typically have greater reliability and validity than a projective measure. Objective tests are usually based on empirical data rather than theory. Many objective tests try to measure aspects of one's personality. The most widely used personality inventory in the United States is the Minnesota Multiphasic Personality Inventory (MMPI). The MMPI contains a series of statements to which a person responds "true" or "false." The administration, scoring and norms have been standardized. (**Psychological tests**)

28. Sometimes. An IQ score, which is a score on an intelligence test, predicts academic performance. There is much debate about the nature of intelligence and it is important to remember that IQ tests do not necessarily measure intelligence. IQ tests tap into various cognitive tasks, but do these tasks represent intelligence? Some theorists believe that intelligence is much more and includes adaptability to the environment and generation of new ideas. Neither of these concepts are measured by IQ tests. (**Psychological tests**)

29. Neuropsychological tests assess brain and nervous system functioning by testing performance on certain tasks. Individuals are tested on their language abilities, attention, memory, motor skills, perceptual skills, and learning. Brain dysfunction is assessed by observing a person's ability to perform certain tasks. Some tests allow the clinician to determine the exact location of the dysfunction. There is some overlap between intelligence tests and neuropsychological tests. These tests tend to be reliable and valid. However, these tests require many hours to administer and are not used unless brain damage is suspected. (**Neuropsychological tests**)

Grade Yourself

Circle the numbers of the questions you missed, then fill in the total incorrect for each topic. If you answered more than three questions incorrectly, you need to focus on that topic. (If a topic has fewer than three questions and you had at least one wrong, we suggest you study that topic also. Read your textbook or a review book, or ask your teacher for help.)

Subject: Clinical Assessment

Topic	Question Numbers	Number Incorrect
Assessment concepts	1, 2, 3, 11, 12, 20	
Clinical interviews	4, 5, 6, 13, 14, 15, 16, 21, 22	
Psychological tests	7, 8, 9, 18, 25, 26, 27, 28	
Neuropsychological tests	10, 19, 29	
Behavioral observations	17, 23, 24	

Interventions

19

Brief Yourself

Insight therapies share an assumption that behavior becomes disordered because we are not aware of what motivates us. Psychoanalysis emphasizes the past, while humanist and existential approaches emphasize the present. *Psychoanalysis* tries to uncover childhood repressions. Rogers tries to create nonjudgmental environments for therapy that will allow a person to become self-actualized. Both existentialists and humanists believe that people are good and that a client's perceptions must be understood by the therapist. *Gestalt therapy* focuses on current needs and the acceptance of responsibility for behavior. *Cognitive-behavior therapy* tries to apply learning principles to psychopathology. *Counterconditioning* substitutes a desirable response in the presence of a stimulus that previously elicited an undesirable response. The token economy is an example of applying operant conditioning principles to changing behavior. *Modeling* is useful in eliminating fears and teaching new behaviors. *Cognitive restructuring* tries to modify thoughts that underlie problem behaviors. Group therapy involves the treatment of several individuals by one therapist. In couples and family therapy, couples and sometimes their children have joint therapy sessions.

Test Yourself

Define the terms in questions 1–10.

1. Psychoanalytic therapy

2. Free association

3. Latent content

4. Client-centered therapy

5. Empathy

6. Counterconditioning

7. REBT

8. T-groups

9. Conjoint therapy

10. Competence

Questions 11–29 are true-false.

11. The two main types of insight therapies are psychoanalytic and behavior therapy.

12. The basic assumption of any therapy is that nonverbal and verbal exchanges between therapist and client in a trusting relationship can help the client achieve various goals.

13. Insight therapy assumes that thoughts, emotions and behaviors become problematic because people do not understand their motivations.

14. Psychoanalytic theory states that normally repressed material can enter consciousness during sleep because the ego defenses are relaxed.

15. The latent content of the dream is what we actually see when we dream and may be a compromise between unconscious desires and the ego.

16. Conditional positive regard means that the therapist accepts the client as a person worthy of dignity and respect, regardless of the client's behavior.

17. Empathy involves feeling pity for a person.

18. Existentialism may be thought of as gloomier than humanism, stressing the anxiety present in making important decisions.

19. Gestalt therapy assumes that all of us bring all of our needs and wants to every situation.

20. Token economies build upon the classical conditioning research.

21. Perls proposed that we learn by watching and imitating others.

22. Modeling is a crucial component of social learning theory.

23. REBT has been found to reduce general anxiety and test anxiety.

24. The goal of Ellis's therapy is to help the client have experiences that will disconfirm their negative conclusions.

25. Social pressures in group are as strong as outside of group.

26. Couples therapy can only treat heterosexual couples.

27. Evaluation of conjoint therapy finds it to be more effective than individual therapy.

28. The insanity defense is plead in about 20 percent of all cases that reach trial and is usually successful.

29. Civil commitment affects a greater number of people than criminal commitment.

30. What are insight therapies?

31. Describe psychoanalytic therapy.

32. Discuss humanistic therapies.

33. How are psychoanalytic and humanistic therapies different?

34. Are there any other insight therapies?

35. What are cognitive-behavior therapies?

36. Describe counterconditioning.

37. Discuss the token economy.

38. What is modeling?

39. Discuss cognitive restructuring.

40. Are there other cognitive therapies?

41. What is group therapy?

42. Discuss couples and family therapy.

43. What is the difference between criminal and civil commitment?

Check Yourself

1. Psychoanalytic therapy tries to assist patients in removing earlier repression and facing childhood conflicts in order to reach a resolution of that conflict. (**Insight therapies**)

2. Free association encourages patients to freely say whatever comes to mind, without censorship. (**Insight therapies**)

3. Latent content of dreams refers to the symbolic nature of the dream which attempts to hide our unconscious desires. (**Insight therapies**)

4. Client-centered therapy is the best known humanistic therapeutic approach and was developed by Carl Rogers. (**Insight therapies**)

5. Empathy is being able to take the perspective or viewpoint of the clients. (**Insight therapies**)

6. Counterconditioning eliminates a response to a specific stimulus when it is replaced by a new response in the presence of the same stimulus. (**Cognitive-behavior therapies**)

7. Rational emotive therapy helps clients challenge beliefs and teaches them how to substitute rational thoughts. (**Cognitive-behavior therapies**)

8. Sensitivity training groups arose from the encounter groups of the 60's and 70's and promote personal growth and understanding in people. (**Group, couples, and family therapy**)

9. In conjoint therapy, partners are in therapy sessions together. (**Group, couples, and family therapy**)

10. Competence is a legal term used to determine if someone is competent to stand trial, meaning they can understand the legal proceedings and aid in their own defense. (**Legal issues**)

11. **False.** The two main types of insight therapies are psychoanalytic and humanistic therapy. (**Insight therapies**)

12. **True.** The basic assumption of any therapy is that nonverbal and verbal exchanges between therapist and client in a trusting relationship can help the client achieve various goals. (**Insight therapies**)

13. **True.** Insight therapy assumes that thoughts, emotions and behaviors become problematic because people do not understand their motivations. (**Insight therapies**)

14. **True.** Psychoanalytic theory states that normally repressed material can enter consciousness during sleep because the ego defenses are relaxed. (**Insight therapies**)

15. **False.** The *manifest* content of the dream is what we actually see when we dream and may be a compromise between unconscious desires and the ego. (**Insight therapies**)

16. **False.** *Unconditional* positive regard means that the therapist accepts the client as a person worthy of dignity and respect, regardless of his or her behavior. (**Insight therapies**)

17. **False.** *Sympathy* involves feeling pity for a person. (**Insight therapies**)

18. **True.** Existentialism may be thought of as gloomier than humanism, stressing the anxiety present in making important decisions. **(Insight therapies)**

19. **True.** Gestalt therapy assumes that all of us bring all of our needs and wants to every situation. **(Insight therapies)**

20. **False.** Token economies build upon the operant conditioning research. **(Cognitive behavior therapies)**

21. **False.** *Bandura* proposed that we learn by watching and imitating others. **(Cognitive behavior therapies)**

22. **True.** Modeling is a crucial component of social learning theory. **(Cognitive behavior therapies)**

23. **True.** REBT has been found to reduce general anxiety and test anxiety. **(Cognitive behavior therapies)**

24. **False.** The goal of *Beck's* therapy is to help the client have experiences that will disconfirm his or her negative conclusions. **(Cognitive behavior therapies)**

25. **True.** Social pressures in group are as strong as outside of group. **(Group, couples, and family therapy)**

26. **False.** Couples therapy can include any couple in a relationship, gay or heterosexual. **(Group, couples, and family therapy)**

27. **True.** Evaluation of conjoint therapy finds it to be more effective than individual therapy. **(Group, couples, and family therapy)**

28. **False.** The insanity defense is plead in about 2 percent of all cases that reach trial and is rarely successful. **(Legal issues)**

29. **True.** Civil commitment affects a greater number of people than criminal commitment. **(Legal issues)**

30. The two main types of insight therapies are psychoanalytic and humanistic therapy. The basic assumption of any therapy is that nonverbal and verbal exchanges between therapist and client in a trusting relationship can help the client achieve various goals. Insight therapy assumes that thoughts, emotions and behaviors become problematic because people do not understand their motivations. Insight therapy tries to help clients become aware of why they think, feel and behave as they do. It is assumed that this increased awareness leads to greater control and enhances adaptive thoughts, emotions and behaviors. **(Insight therapies)**

31. Psychoanalytic therapy is the most common approach to psychopathology and its treatment. Sigmund Freud developed psychoanalytic theory and the psychoanalytic approach to therapy. Freud believed that the most important determinants of behavior are unconscious and that behavior results from an interaction between our id, ego and superego. Psychoanalytic therapy tries to assist patients in removing earlier repression and facing childhood conflicts in order to reach a resolution of that conflict. Repression prevents the ego from properly developing as the individual ages. In order for the ego to fully mature, the repression must be overcome. The best known technique is free association which encourages patients to freely say whatever comes to mind, without censorship. Another technique that is used is dream analysis. Psychoanalytic theory states that normally repressed material can enter consciousness during sleep because the ego defenses are relaxed. Because this material is disturbing to us, it usually appears disguised in our dreams. Dreams must be analyzed for symbolic content that may reveal repressed desires. The latent content of dreams refers to the symbolic nature of the dream trying to hide our unconscious desires. The manifest content of the dream is what we actually see when we dream and may be a compromise between unconscious desires and the ego. **(Insight therapies)**

32. The humanistic approach arose largely as a reaction against psychoanalysis. Abraham Maslow was a pioneer in humanism who had a positive view of human nature. He believed that people are basically healthy and unique with a drive toward self-actualization. Humans by nature are resourceful, active, and good. Suffering is the result of a denial of this basic human goodness. Client-centered therapy is the best known humanistic therapeutic approach and was developed by Carl Rogers. The person seeking therapy is regarded as a client rather than a patient and is responsible for the course of his or her treatment. Therapists create conditions that help clients discover their feelings and make their own decisions. There are three conditions necessary for effective treatment in this approach: empathy, unconditional positive regard and genuineness. Empathy is being able to take the perspective of the clients, to walk a mile in their shoes, so to speak. It is not sympathy which involves feeling pity for a person. Empathy allows the therapist to see the world through the client's eyes. Unconditional positive regard means that the therapist accepts the client as a person worthy of dignity and respect, regardless of the client's behavior. Genuineness is communicated by the therapist who is honest and willing to share some of his or her own experiences when necessary. **(Insight therapies)**

33. Psychoanalytic therapy focuses on the unconscious, seeing the unconscious as controlling much of our behavior; therapists interpret free associations and dreams for the client. Humanistic therapy views people as innately good, aware of their behavior, and goal-directed in their behavior; therapists are nondirective, letting the client direct the flow and course of therapy. **(Insight therapies)**

34. Yes, both gestalt and existential therapies are considered to be insight therapies. Existentialists in this country have included Rollo May and Abraham Maslow. Existentialism emphasizes personal growth, like humanism. Existentialism may be thought of as gloomier than humanism, stressing the anxiety present in making important decisions. Being alive means we have to confront the anxiety that comes from making choices. Existential anxiety comes from several sources: our own mortality, our helplessness in the face of chance or randomness, creating meaning in our lives and the knowledge that each of us is ultimately alone. Existential therapy helps the person explore his or her behavior, face the choices we must make and relate authentically to others. The goal of existential therapy is to make the client aware of his or her potential for growth. Gestalt therapy holds that people are basically good. Psychological problems come from denying this goodness according to Perls, gestalt's major proponent. Gestalt therapy assumes that all of us bring all of our needs and wants to every situation. We project our needs and fears onto our environment. Gestalt therapists may encourage the clients to finish "unfinished business" from the past, which can influence their present functioning. Perls focuses on the here and now and considers each person an actor, being responsible for his or her own behavior. **(Insight therapies)**

35. The focus of cognitive psychology is on how people structure their experiences and how they understand them. The learning process is much more complex than learning theorists once believed. Cognitive psychologists study how we acquire, store, and retrieve information and memories. Techniques that are cognitive or behavioral include counterconditioning (systematic desensitization or token economies), modeling, and cognitive restructuring. **(Cognitive-behavior therapies)**

36. Counterconditioning eliminates a response to a specific stimulus when it is replaced by a new response in the presence of the same stimulus. This may help treat phobias by replacing a fear response with a non-fear response to a specific stimulus. Wolpe applied the technique of counterconditioning to adults with phobias referring to it as systematic desensitization. Wolpe taught his patients to use deep muscle relaxation and imagine the feared object. The relaxation inhibited the anxiety response. Over time, a client can imagine increasingly anxiety provoking situations and tolerate them without any anxiety. **(Cognitive-behavior therapies)**

37. Token economies build upon the operant conditioning research. Tokens are earned by positive behaviors and can be exchanged for privileges and objects. The rules for getting tokens and buying items with

tokens are clearly established and publicized. The aim was to increase certain behaviors by rewarding them and decrease others by not being rewarded. **(Cognitive-behavior therapies)**

38. Modeling is a crucial component of social learning theory. Bandura proposed that we learn by watching and imitating others. Witnessing a model perform a behavior will influence our own behavior. When we see a model being reinforced for behavior, we are more likely to engage in that behavior. If we see a model being punished for a behavior, then we are less likely to engage in that behavior. **(Cognitive-behavior therapies)**

39. Cognitive-behavior therapists try to alter the thought processes of clients in order to change their emotions and behavior. One major cognitive therapist, Albert Ellis, believes that maladaptive feelings and behaviors are the result of irrational beliefs. An example of an irrational belief is thinking that you must be perfect in every way. Ellis' therapy, rational emotive therapy (REBT), helps patients challenge beliefs and teaches them how to substitute rational thoughts. People can have many irrational beliefs, including the idea that one has to be perfect and one must be loved by everyone. REBT has been found to reduce general anxiety and test anxiety. REBT may be useful in treating anger. **(Cognitive-behavior therapies)**

40. Yes, Beck's cognitive therapy focuses on the negative patterns in which people think about themselves and the world. These negative thoughts are maintained by errors in logic. The goal of this therapy is to help the client have experiences that will disconfirm their negative conclusions. **(Cognitive-behavior therapies)**

41. Group therapy involves treating several individuals at the same time. Group members learn vicariously from each other. Social pressures in group are as strong as outside of group. Also, groups allow people to discover that others have problems similar to their own. Virtually all techniques used for individual therapy can be used in groups. T-groups, sensitivity training groups, arose from the encounter groups of the 60's and 70's. The T-group is educational and not for the most severe psychoses. T-groups promote personal growth and understanding in people. Group desensitization can be used to treat many people deep muscle relaxation and anxiety hierarchies simultaneously. Social skills can also be taught in groups of clients who have similar skill deficits. Evaluations of group therapy have demonstrated that group therapies appear to have beneficial effects, dependent people do better in structured groups, cohesive groups lead to better results than noncohesive groups, and negative feedback is effective when accompanied by positive feedback. **(Group, couples, and family therapy)**

42. Couples therapy can include any couple in a relationship (gay or heterosexual, married or not) and may sometime necessitate involving the children. Most professionals who conduct couples therapy also conduct family therapy. Conflict inevitably arises in any long-term relationship. The way in which couples deal with conflict determines the quality and duration of their relationship. Some couples avoid acknowledging conflict, but resentments build and these partners may drift apart emotionally. Although the focus of these types of therapy is on at least two family members, there is no set procedure or technique for conjoint therapy. Most couples therapy is conjoint, partners together in therapy session. Distressed couples do not react positively to this process. In all forms of couples therapy, each partner is trained to listen empathically to the other, to state clearly what he or she heard and what the feelings underlying the statements are. Patterns of communication may be studied using videotapes of the couples interactions at home. Evaluation of conjoint therapy finds it to be more effective than individual therapy and that therapy results are better for younger couples and when no steps toward divorce are taken. **(Group, couples, and family therapy)**

43. Mentally ill people who have committed a crime can be committed to a prison hospital through criminal commitment proceedings. The insanity defense is plead in about 2 percent of all cases that reach trial and is rarely successful. Criminal law rests on the assumption that people have free will and when someone

breaks the law it is because they have chosen to do so. Those who are judged insane are presumed to have less responsibility for their actions because they are unable to distinguish right from wrong or they have a mental defect. Insanity is a legal term, not a psychological term. Another legal term, competence, is used to determine if someone is competent to stand trial, meaning they can understand the legal proceedings and aid in their own defense. Civil commitment affects a greater number of people than criminal commitment. In most states, people can be committed to a hospital against their will if they are mentally ill and a danger to themselves or others. There are formal and informal procedures for commitment. Formal commitment is by court order and can be requested by any citizen. Informal or emergency commitment can be accomplished without a court order. Typically, two physicians are needed to sign a commitment order than can range from 24 hours to 20 days. (**Legal issues**)

Grade Yourself

Circle the numbers of the questions you missed, then fill in the total incorrect for each topic. If you answered more than three questions incorrectly, you need to focus on that topic. (If a topic has fewer than three questions and you had at least one wrong, we suggest you study that topic also. Read your textbook or a review book, or ask your teacher for help.)

Subject: Interventions

Topic	Question Numbers	Number Incorrect
Insight therapies	1, 2, 3, 4, 5, 11, 12, 13, 14, 15, 16, 17, 18, 19, 30, 31, 32, 33, 34	
Cognitive-behavior therapies	6, 7, 20, 21, 22, 23, 24, 35, 36, 37, 38, 39, 40	
Group, couples, and family therapy	8, 9, 25, 26, 27, 41, 42	
Legal issues	10, 28, 29, 43	